my city need something

portraits and prose for black existence

Christopher R. Rogers and karim brown

my city need something

portraits and prose for black existence

Christopher R. Rogers and karim brown

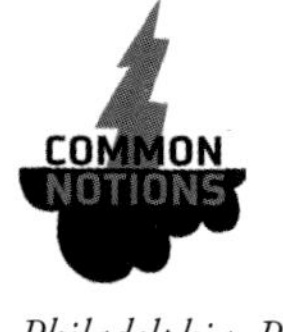

Philadelphia, PA

My City Need Something: Portraits and Prose for Black Existence

ISBN: 978-1-945335-50-1 | eBook ISBN: 978-1-945335-71-6

10 9 8 7 6 5 4 3 2 1

Common Notions
PO Box 18823
Philadelphia, PA 19119

www.commonnotions.org
info@commonnotions.org

Discounted bulk quantities of our books are available for organizing, educational, or fundraising purposes. Please contact Common Notions at the address above for more information.

Photography by karim brown
Cover design by Josh MacPhee
Layout design by Christopher R. Rogers and karim brown
Typesetting by Sydney Rainer

contents

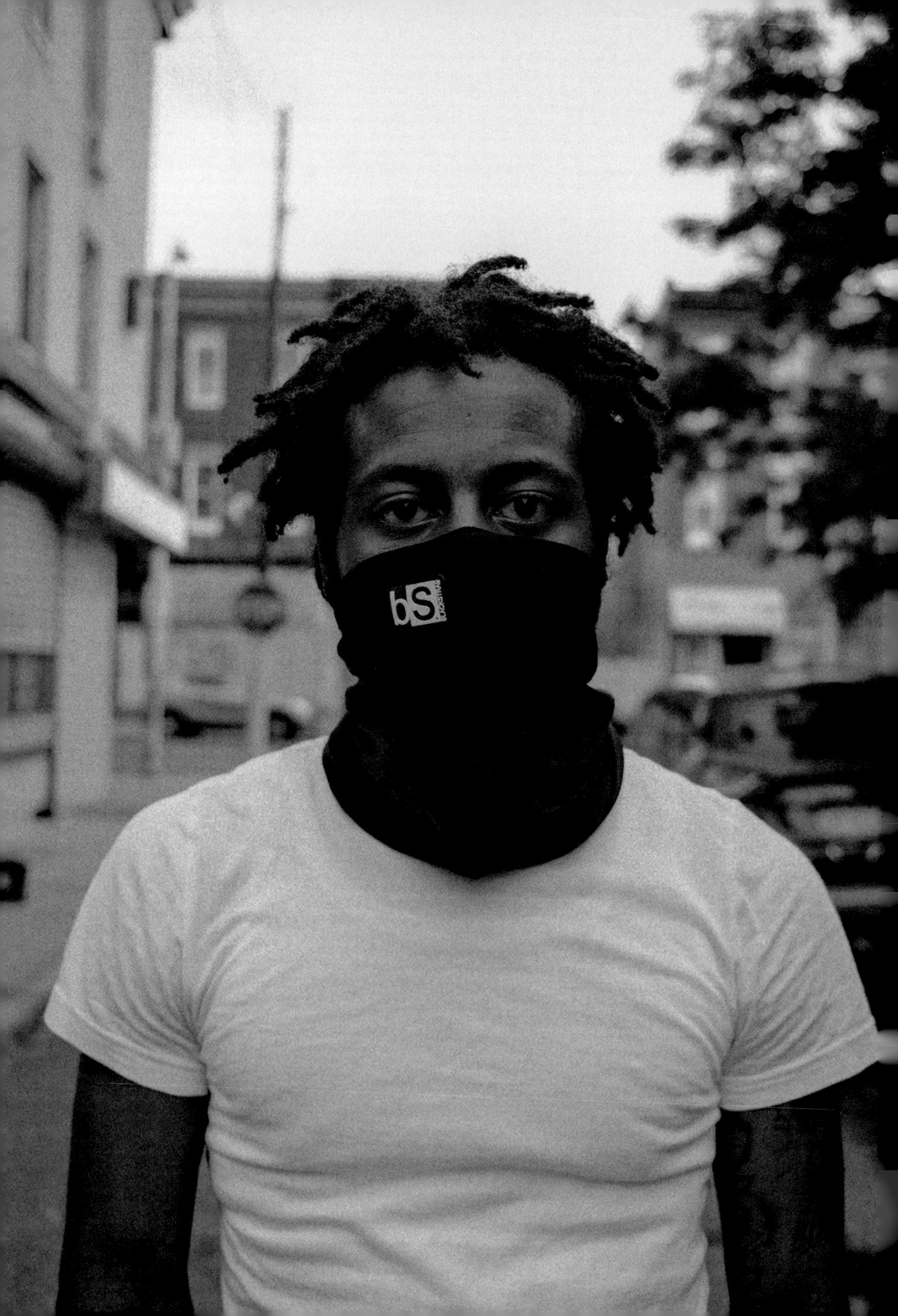
bS

a declaration of self-defense

This is just a foreword. We consider ourselves fully committed. We are sure that other young people like us exist prepared to add their signatures to ours and who—to the extent that it remains compatible with continuing to live—refuse to become part of the surrounding ignominy. And we've had it with those who try, consciously or not, with smiles, work, exactitude, proprieties, speeches, writing, actions, and with their very being, to make us believe that things can continue as they are. We are hell-bent on sincerity. We want to see clearly into our dreams, and we are listening to what they tell us. **This little storybook is a provisional tool, and if it collapses, we shall find others.** If it is especially aimed at young Blacks, it is because we consider that they in particular suffer from the effects of capitalism (apart from Africa, witness Haiti, witness Scottsboro, witness Broad and Erie, witness 52nd and Market, witness Pastorius and Baynton, witness ________, witness our city) and that they seem to offer—in having a materially defined ethnic personality—a generally higher potential for revolt and joy. We are speaking to those who are not already branded as killed, established, fucked-up, academic, successful, decorated, decayed, provided for, decorative, prudish opportunists. We are speaking to those who can still accept life with some appearance of truthfulness. We do not accept that we should be ashamed of what we suffer. And all those who adopt the same attitude, no matter where they come from, will find they are welcome among us.

—Christopher R. Rogers and karim brown

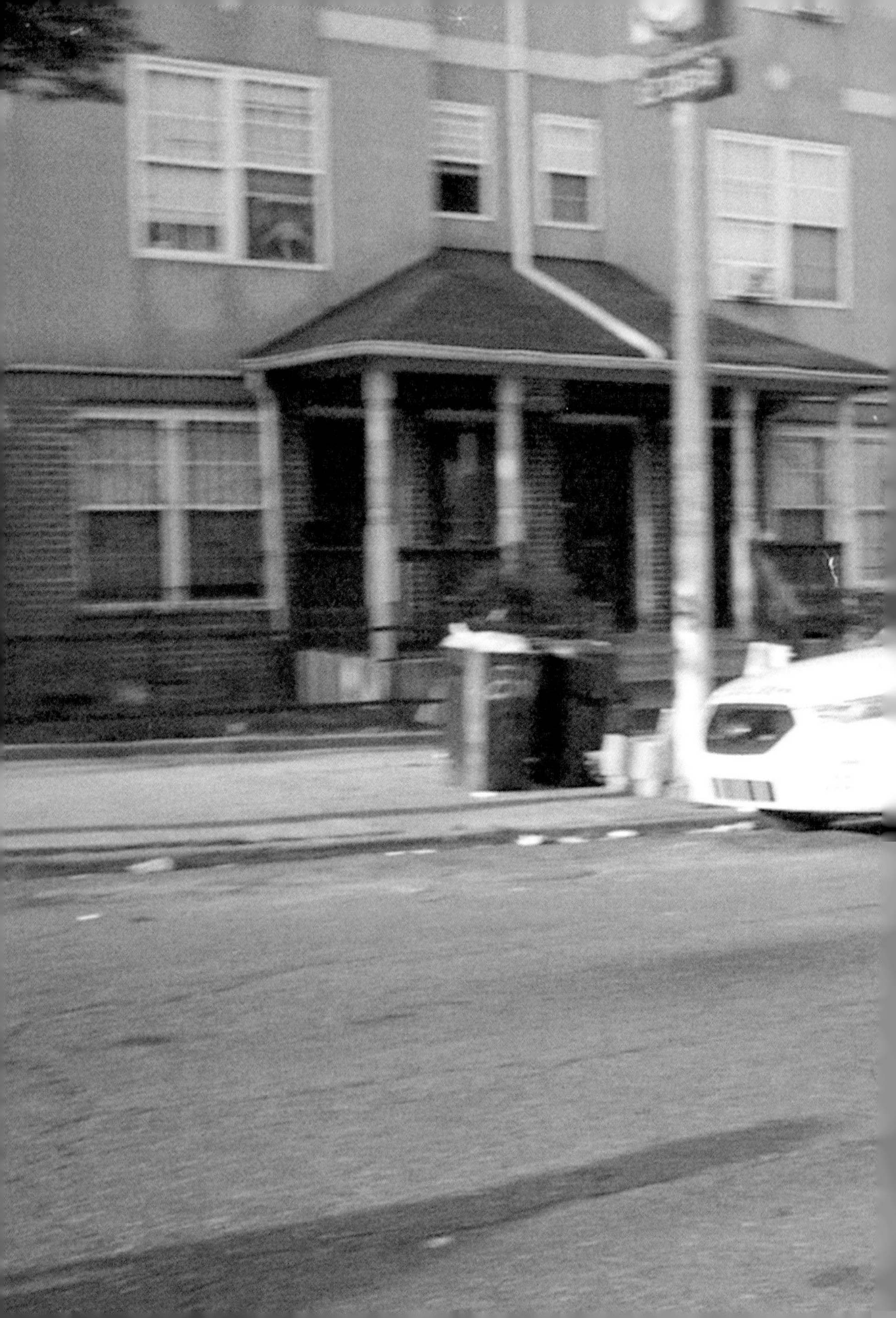

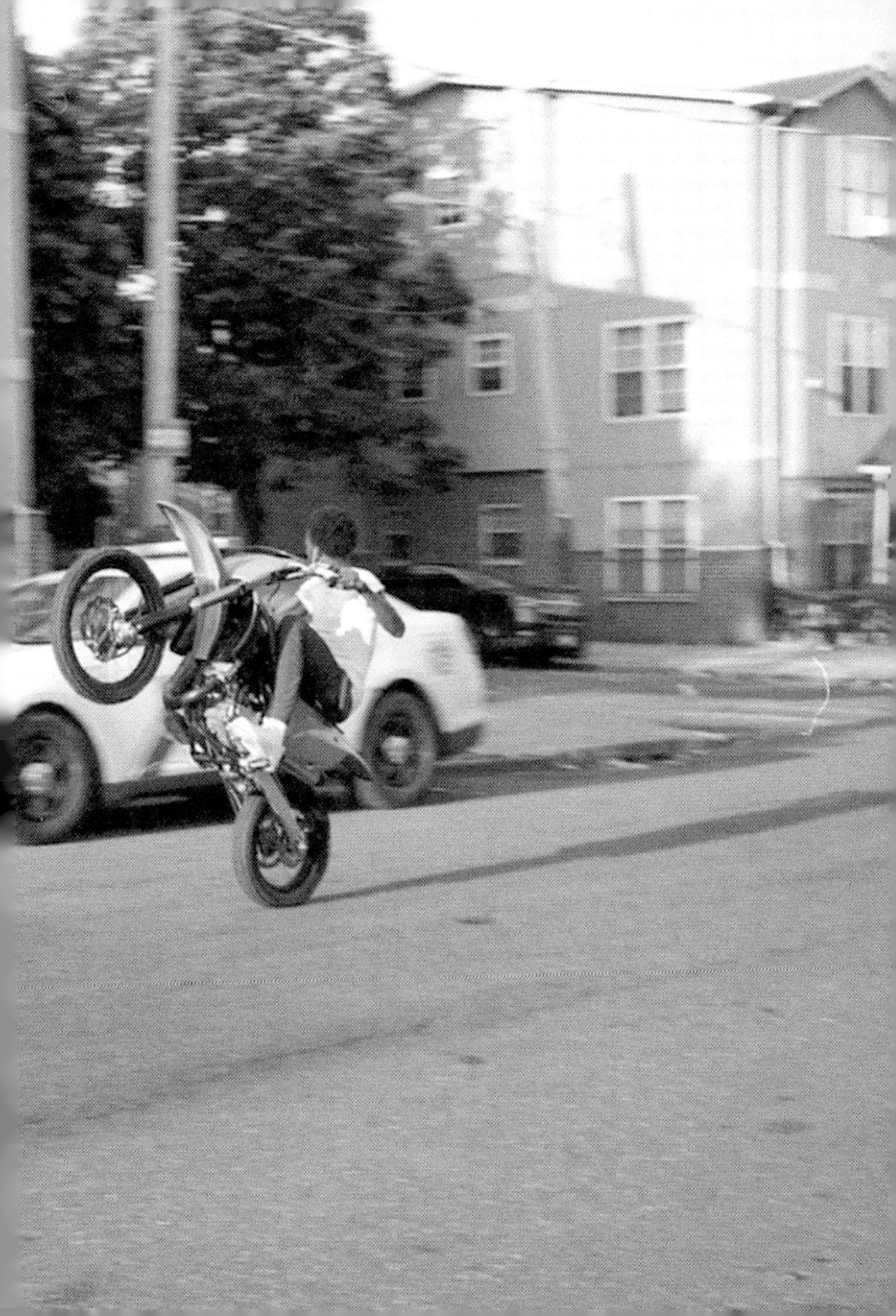

a note on methods, man

In those days it was either live with music or die with noise, and we chose rather desperately to live.

–Ralph Ellison, *Living with Music*

I listen to some music that I love, and it inspires me to write a poem. My poem is not going to be that music. And if my poem only attempts to imitate that music, it's not going to be worth a lot. But if it's an attempt to get at what is essential to that music, perhaps it will approach the secret of that music . . . .

—Fred Moten, "'Words Don't Go There': An Interview with Fred Moten"

Welcome to *my city need something*, our loving response to our beloved new ancestor Rakim "PnB Rock" Allen, who was taken from us too soon to be able to build with Us on it without y'all, if only on this hellish earthly plane.

In Cherelle Parker's "One Philadelphia," there's a lot that going on, bruh, but it's mostly the changing same you always sung about. What I wanna do is simply be in convo with you about what I think is going on, what I believe addresses the needs of this city that you and us both grieve and will always continue to suffer from. I hope I'm not coming across as enlightened. That definitely ain't my goal. I'm just trying to be real. I'm just trying to answer the call.

I just feel that we all get stuck sometime, like you were when you made the track "My City Need Something." That's why I know it worked. It resonated. Because when I heard it, I was living in North Philly myself, ordering delivery from your fantastic Burger Lane off 22nd Street, and feeling stuck too. It came from a real place; *we know this place*, like Mama Sunni Patterson said. We all know.

Just to keep it a bean, I'm really from Chester. I might sometimes be confusing Diamond Street realities with long 9th Street memories.

I hope what I offer here serves as a loving reminder of the light that I know exists in you, in Us. This is not one of those Nathaniel Mackey hoodoo tricks where I'm really just speaking to the future reader, using you as one of the subversive epistolary mechanisms that allows me, the author, to get the point across better. He was imagining music then; I'm working with a real song here.

I'm truly seeking right relationship with you, my brother. In that, it's no point in me doing this without also putting myself on the line some. NTanya Lee once said to me, "You got to extend trust to build trust."

I'll be attempting to color how my own personal contradictions, mistakes, and desires must someway contribute to an answer worth all of us writing down, all of Us gathering about, regarding your previously established plea for some knowledge of what if anything could be done to free us from this suffering. That's what you meant, right?

How else do I stand to rest my case, which reflects Zora Neale Hurston's folk-documented assertion that *we win from within*? I aim to show my work, even if I'm unfinished and incomplete, or precisely because so, I might just be bestowed some loving correction from you and others along the way. Help me help you help Us get to this place of freedom. Together.

Another hardworking poet like you, PnB, once stated:

> *This poem has four reasons for being. One, it is a poem of desperation. Two, it is a poem for those who would like to be reminded. Three, it is a poem for those who would like NOT to be reminded. Four, it is a poem to inform those who don't know.*
>
> —Amir Sulaiman, "Dead Man Walking"

He was saying his poems. I'm saying my little essays you will find here. I'm nobody's poet. They care about things that I don't even care to know. I might call them "short stories" if they were actually short, and I'd felt I could make Henry Dumas and Pat Chamoiseau proud, could make Toni Cade Bambara smile, could make John Edgar Wideman offer a Black fatherly nod of approval from the playground ball-court benches.

Yet, Rock, I gotta take a step back to say that this whole experiment is really about practicing striving. And striving is an important, meaningful muscle we all need to flex more often. So fuck it, I don't mind if you do call them "short stories." Yet, I did feel like I had to live a long life to earn these. Not everybody is promised those. And to be quite honest, most of these so-called short stories reflect lessons I only learned last year, as June Jordan talked about in "Requiem for the Champ." So yeah, call 'em whatever you want; I just have to tell them.

Yes, I know that I am first talking to myself while writing this. I know I would hate to be called anything as silly as the unelected representative of whosoever's collective opinion, including in my own city. But maybe, just maybe, if I can be honest, thoughtful, and caring with myself and others, then perhaps I could land on something that strikes a chord.

Rock, I say what I want for you is what I want for me. We gotta welcome reminders of our marvelous, fragile humanity and the present, ordinary, daily chances for liberation that lie within our becoming. Maya Angelou said, "I am convinced that most people do not grow up." I simply want my voice to echo the chorus of those wise Black grown folks who noticed and nurtured Us, rather than misread and maligned us. I'm choosing to grow up. I'm striving to grow up. I know, for the moment at least, that I want to be well.

> *In storytelling, you can do that—that's why I like storytelling. When you tell a story, you automatically talk about traditions, but they are never separate from the people, the human implications. You're really talking about language, you're talking about politics and morality and economics and culture, and you never have to come out and say you're talking about these things—you don't have to isolate them and therefore freeze them—but you're still talking about them. You're talking about all your connections as a human being. You're talking about many dimensions instead of just one. You don't start with the answers. Someone asked me what answers did I have for such and such a thing. I said that I didn't have any answers. She said that when she read my book she could see answers. She could see I had answers. But you don't start with the answers. I don't start with the answers, I start with the telling, and sometimes the answers come out of the telling.*
>
> —Gayl Jones, "Gayl Jones: An Interview"

But PnB, to start this for real for real, I have to introduce you to our illustrator and also my "we know the answers do exist" codefendant karim brown, the documentary photographer who will be providing the impressive evidence in the form of inspired portraits of Philadelphia's Black social life as it exists here in the 215, in a register of Black existence that reaches beyond both the undue imposed suffering and the reactionary, always-on, instant, guerilla, political resistance stunts too. That loud stuff. You know our people don't be taking nothing serious. I'm more talking about the sovereignty of quiet. The Sovereignty of the

Imagination. Reminds me: one of the recent bombs karim dropped on me was: "If we are fighting or 'rebelling' all of the time, when are we living?" Boom. That's my man, karim. You gotta meet him, bro.

Dawoud Bey teaches us about striving of the Black photographer when he says:

> *Making art always involves being able to manifest an idea, in photography's case, making it visible. You use the camera to transform what you see into a new experience, anticipating the image you wish to make but also being open to chance or external elements that could transform the image and your expectations.*

We must manifest and improvise the image of the world for our own eyes and respiratory systems so that we will once and for all be able to witness breathing within our free-and-still-goin'-be-fragile Black lives.

This requires refusing easy victories and getting comfortable with the discomfort of there being no lasting guarantees on this planet. We're forever in motion—tidalectically. We must endlessly search for that freedom, form its shape and contours from the depth of our experiences and the boundlessness of our imaginations. If we can come up with such a resonant question of our time like you did for us, PnB, I believe we do have a duty to recover or invent some answers. Of course, this is just one way of seeing it, but I do believe it to be the most worthwhile, interesting, gallant way of responding—with our lives. Toni Morrison taught me that word, *gallant*. I plan to come back to this, and her, in a couple different ways. She's at all times and always important, forever.

I'm interested in investigating and inventing room for free living on our own Black-ass terms. I've found within karim's work a glimpse into everyday Black Philadelphian lifework, as an instance of and insistence upon a striving presence and liberating cultural existence that stands to be realized and synthesized to potentially transform the world around us. Sister Grace and Deacon Jimmy from Detroit say we can't do this work, can't transform this world, without first being willing to transform ourselves.

I'm telling you PnB (can I call you Rock?), there's some working answers out there that we could be practicing on and getting right with, some *something worth holding on to* like the ones Bilal blues'd about. I think he lives up in Germantown too. I saw him in the Germantown and Chelten Avenue CVS one time. That was some time before we all lived in Mayor Cherelle Parker's Philadelphia.

Yeah, it may be obvious to us both that it is not now, nor ever has been, and simply will never be "One Philly." That goal is foolish, off, and most likely harmful in a variety of ways we can no longer handle.

Rock, we must be making room for some interdependent plural possibilities for this city, underwritten by the revolutionary love our everyday choices may stand to nurture within us for sharing with each other, the land, and life itself.

So, of course, to make this experimental design of a dialogue between us a bit more rigorous, I gave karim the final say on all the images. It's only right. If he didn't budge, I didn't push. I had to really work with them, struggle with them and myself on how to grasp the ordinary opportunities for practicing Black liberation that undoubtedly gotta be alive within each one of them. Because they are images of Us.

I been listening to these images, Rock. Sometimes I had to search those lower frequencies that Ralph Ellison told us existed (and then maybe he forgot about? That's what Larry Neal from North Philly said.) Really, I, Curtis Mayfield stared and stared until I came up with something; not something imagined, but something real. Something like your song. Which to say, one mo' time, that I know these worldmaking-otherwise possibilities don't just exist in me. We both gotta know that I'm really not that special. None of Us are individually. But I know it's working on me to do something that feels a bit more free. To practice something different. I feel a bit more responsible for facing up to what's killing me; I may be getting high off my own supply.

This visual mixtape serves to lovingly remind you, Rock, and the rest of Us too, that working answers for our shared liberation do exist around here, however uniquely textured they are by our identities and upbringings in this chaos of a world. I often recite that Septima Clark taught us that chaos is a gift and the gift it creates is beautiful thinking. And this year, the fifth since the Uprising of 2020 in which we having this grounding, brother, it ain't nothing but chaos. We just got to tell our stories. Mama Gwendolyn Brooks say we owe honest reporting.

So the final good/bad news, Rock, is YES—we owe it to all of our folk here and gone to reclaim our ancestrally derived working answers to shape and explore some kind of lifework worth living, putting them and Us to work endlessly in service of us all, transforming ourselves and the world through committed practice and critical reflection. None of us are off the hook. Even when we sometimes forget and consent to inviting somebody who really strives to love Us to offer a timely reminder that we will remain not no better than what we practice.

Now, for this life that was coming, he had to prepare himself. It was not easy. He had to think of a place of his own now. He had to think of where his life had gone. He had to think of a new beginning. He had to think of forgiveness. He had to think of the scriptures, of the part that said, Lord, how many times shall my brother offend me? And try to understand the meaning of unto seventy everlasting times seven, to understand that his brother's and his own sin and forgiveness was an ongoing wrestling between human frailty and God's grace, a cycle of violation and restoration, of injury and healing as the lot of mankind. He had to think and work things out. He had to find meaning in his captivity, his enslavement, his enduring, to re-examine his relationship with women, his role as a man, he had to think of power, of what it was, of what must be its function. He had to think of the world, of life, what was it, was it a matter of domination by the strongest, what was man, what was tribe and people and race and country? He had to re-examine all the old questions, to look again at the old songs, the old sayings, the stories,—the meanings. And he had to be careful about looking. back to what things might have been. He had to look towards the future. He had to find the elation, the zeal for this new life. For, what he had woken up into was a new world.

—Earl Lovelace, *Salt*

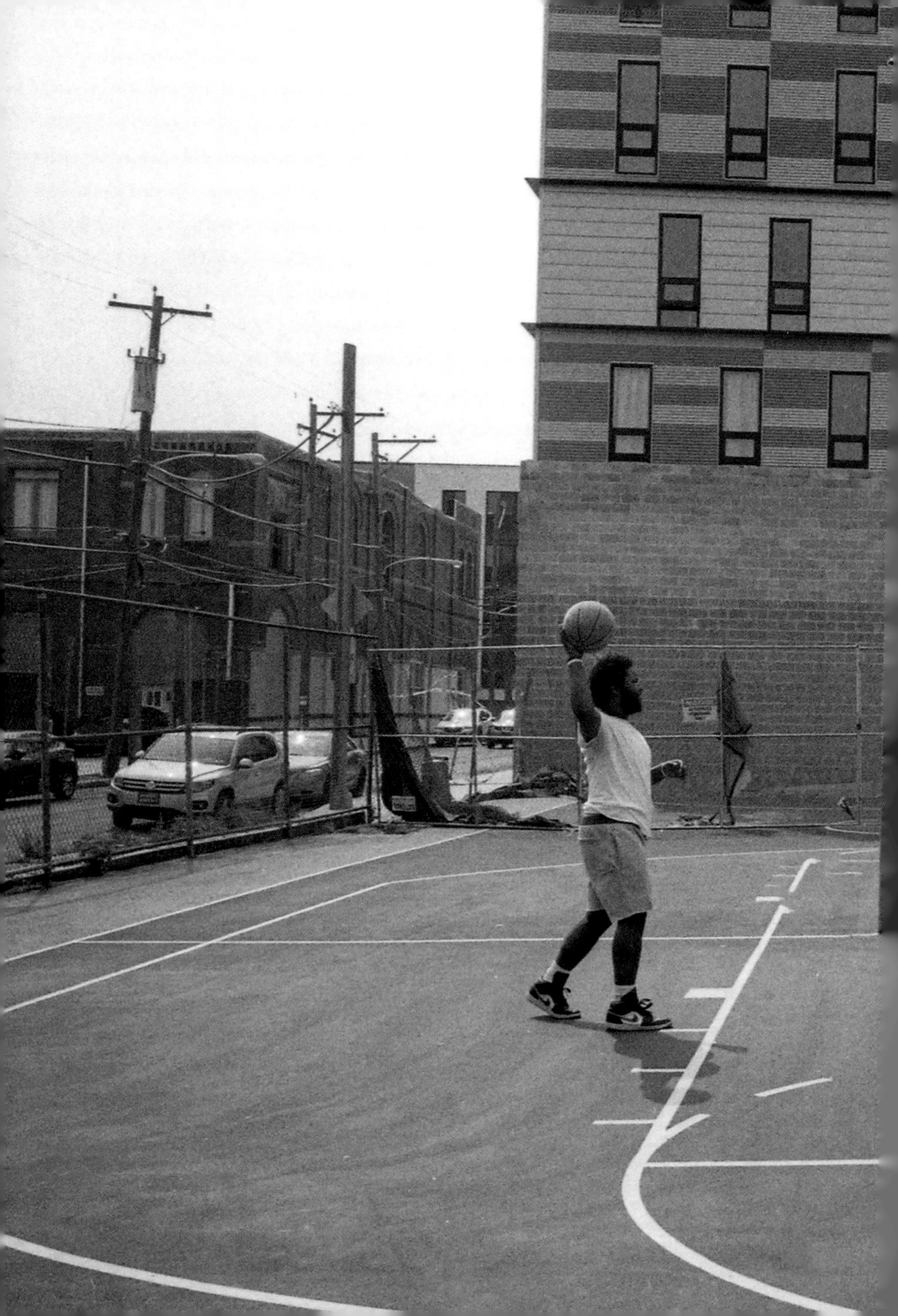

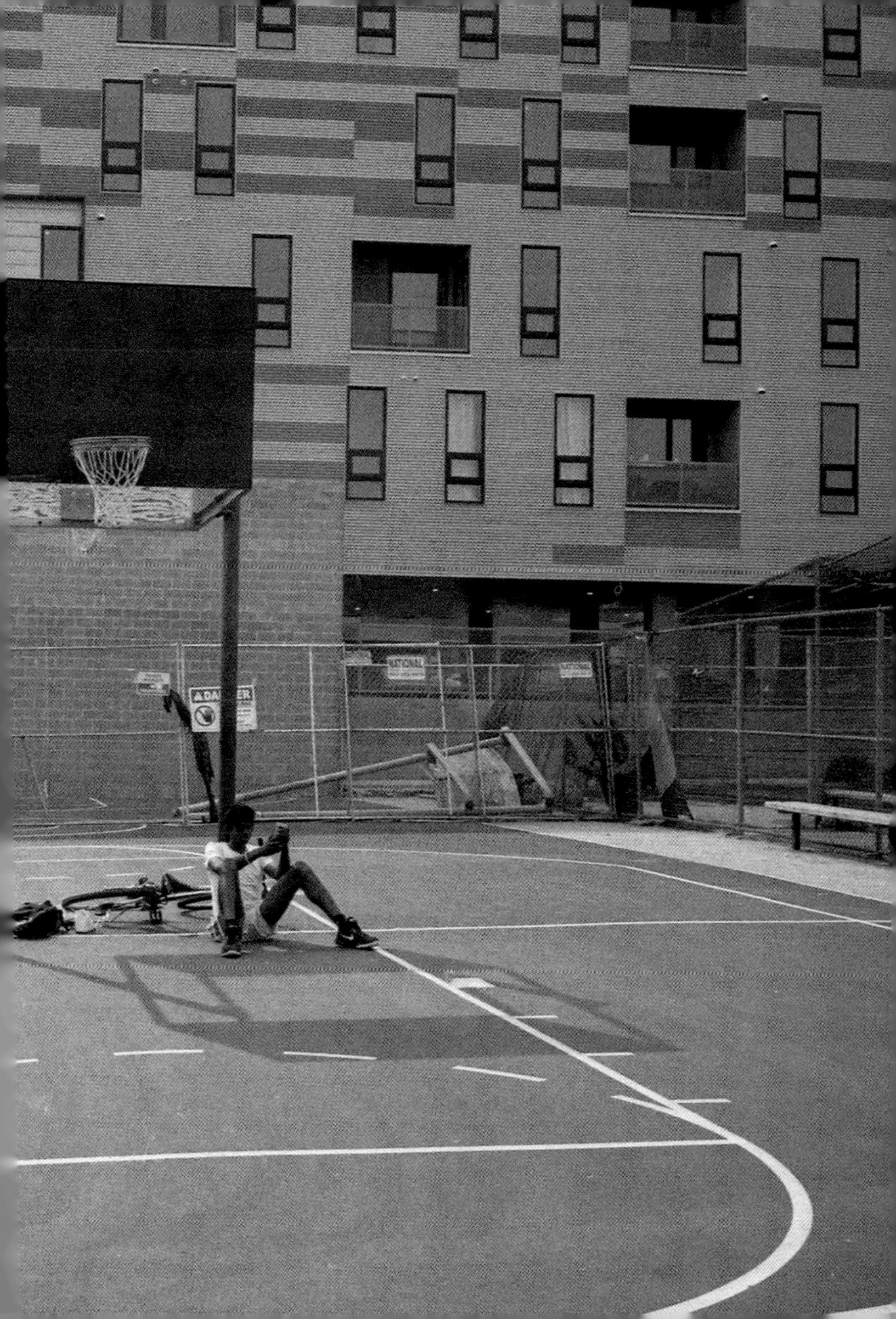

we remain not no better than what we practice

And I don't know what it is but my city need something . . . I swear we need something different but I don't know what it is.

—Rakim "PnB Rock" Allen

Any ordinary day offers an opportunity to practice freedom, to create revolution internally, to rehearse for governance . . . .

—Toni Cade Bambara

I'm just saying. I don't know for real for real, Rock, but I have a genuine, some-type-of-liberating feeling that *we do know*. We do know that the answer for our city, what we need, something different is already out there, maybe even somewhere in here with Us right now too. We just got to take a look around and practice being an honest witness to our surroundings.

Because I for damn sure know we at least got some working answers up on the shelf of the Home of Black Books aka Hakim's Bookstore. Maybe not readymade, enduring solutions for everyone, but some pretty useful starting templates we can remix, *feel*, and groove into a kind of provisional infrastructure for something otherwise yet to come.

I definitively know that them kind of answers already been sent; our ancestors did their big one for Us. I know that at the bare minimum, even if I hadn't yet today hit the streets and checked the mail. You know we had some praying grandmothers.

I can't call it, but I feel like the question underneath your question is whether we, mere everyday people, are truly willing to sacrifice and unlearn what we know. We must, in order to address those needs we pretending we don't know today. What if it is true that everything must go? Are we willing to chalk it? Do we really walk daily down Pastorius, Baynton, and all the other Philly backblocks knowing we have nothing to lose but our chains? Do we know what it requires of Us to live out life from that precious mustard seed of grounded truth?

You should know now when I say "WE," I don't just simply mean the collective all-of-y'all *we*, but more intimately the heart of that diasporic Black *we*-ness that is found within the residue of any one of all of Us. And I'm only trying to talk to Us. I'm only trying to cultivate Us into a revolutionary *we*.

I believe it was Lorraine Hansberry who dramatically said, "In order to make an argument for anything universal, you must pay very great attention to the specific . . ." and I dig it, but I gotta add all its mess too, in the strongest Douglas Kearney sense of the shit. I think us all hold a piece of that messy, marvelous specific; an uncaptive infinity of infinity stones that leverage our power to transform the world.

I believe, naively if you will, that we can choose to pursue and craft our freedom-suite dreams now rather than be subject to provide our soul-power to whatever remains to come in late Babylon's onslaught. I believe we can submit our will to a yearning, to the possibility of a Black future if you will. I believe, when in pursuit of its dungeon-shook-kind-of-Black-truth, we can then decipher actions that it takes to make that future manifest, and then socially regenerate the persistence necessary for the dozens and dozens of mistakes we shall make along the way in attempting to make possible new and freer worlds.

Mistakes that we made because we were guilty of *trying something*, trying to fulfill a dream that existed beyond our pretty little selves, though of course none of Us should be speaking in absolutes. But yeah, most of them were sincere mistakes because we acted, often earnestly and always from a sense of desperation. We may have foolishly fought to embody the free worlds we wanted ourselves to exist within, for however long. We dared to put ourselves on the line for it. We strived. We were forceful and decisive.

Now, Rock, I don't believe any of our strivings require nor guarantee the permanence of these promised material realities of liberation lasting. That's a historical luxury. Yet, I think what's most fulfilling for Us, what makes it such a flex for the soul, is the striving itself. We own the last laugh when we show the world that making a new reality is possible, which is a loud and proud collective investment into thriving Black futures we may never see on this physical plane.

Our promised afterlives may stand a chance; but don't live your life on promises, Rock; they fail and break us often. Focus on life "in the along," as Miss Brooks once said watching out for us from her second-floor Bronzeville apartment. She was always watching, witnessing, looking out for Us.

The most urgent point of all this back and forth is that for us Black folks from the city, my city, our city to truly have an answer for you, our beloved new ancestor Rock, our striving for an otherwise future gotta be what we must rehearse inside ourselves and in public with one another; because we will remain not no better than what we practice. We got to run and tell that to our people. It just may be the only way we gon' stay free out here.

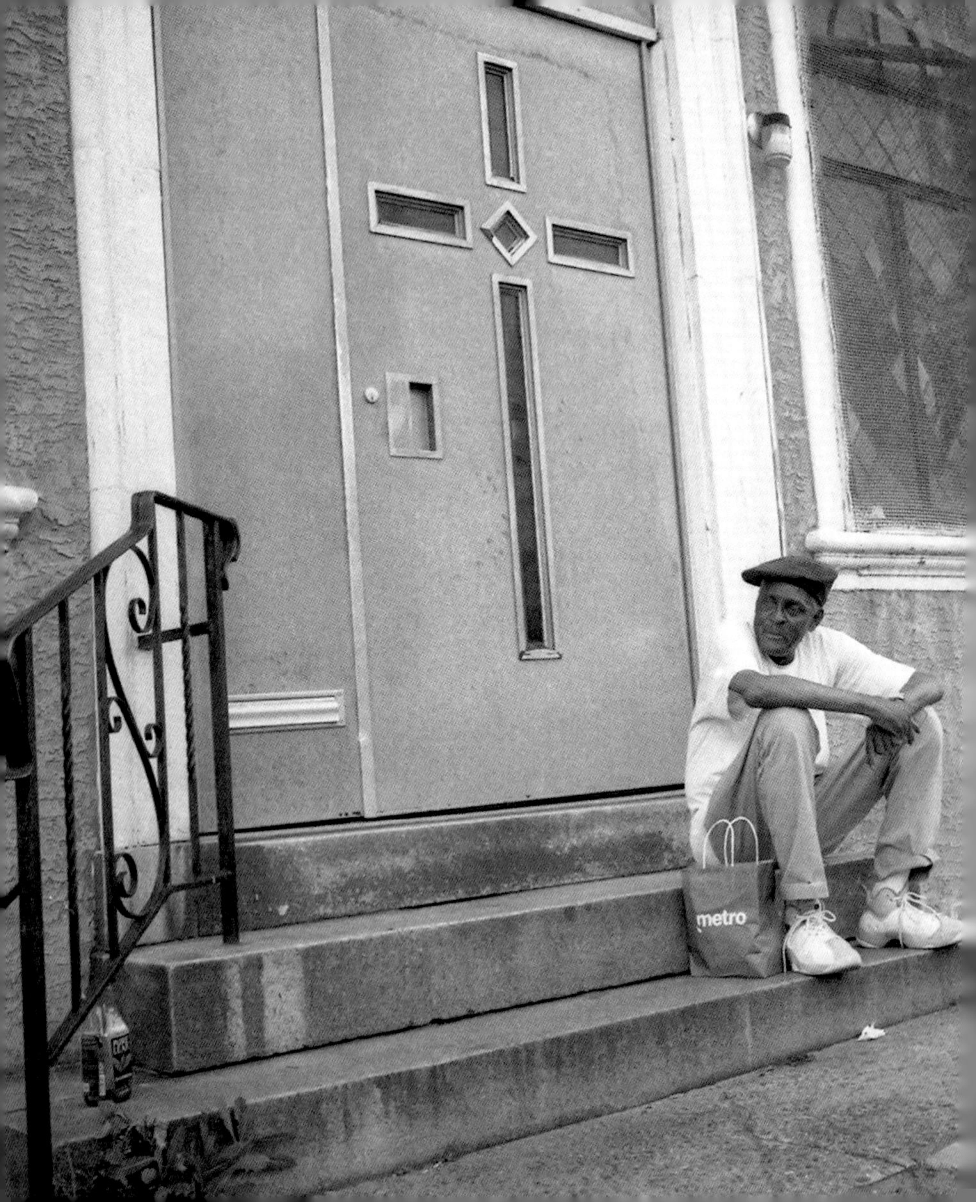
metro

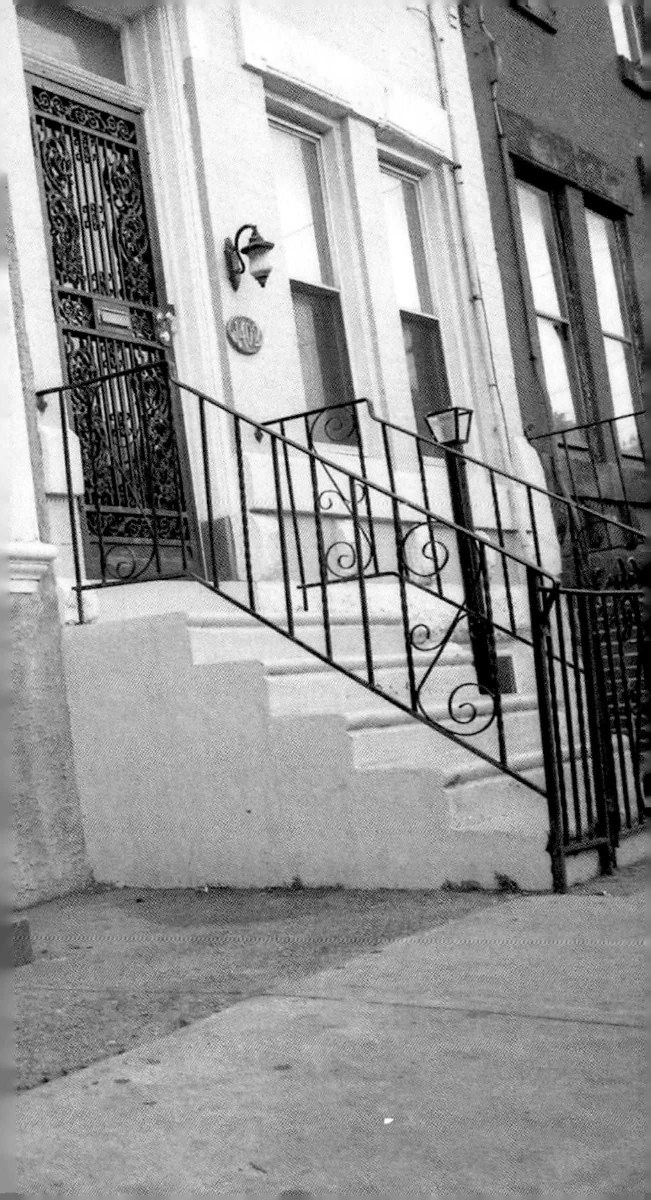

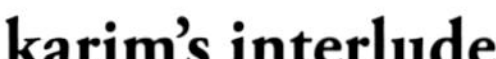

karim's interlude

AGT: *Thinking about time a little more. What are the things that keep you up? Specifically around your photography? Are there ideas that are germinating or moving with you, circulating in your mind that you haven't finalized but are working through?*

kb: *Yes. I am really interested in this beingness, just existing. Like I often imagine myself. [karim's toddler daughter walks in the room and asks to be covered up in bed] I'm often reflecting on moments just like that . . . of walking by with my camera and photographing a dad engaging with his daughter. Like stolen moments like that. What are Black folk doing when we are just sitting still . . . just being. Those are ideas that weigh heavy on my mind. And how I can be better prepared to document them. Also because I can't hit the streets as much I've been appreciating more of what's in front of me. [karim exits to tuck his daughter in] So because I can't hit the streets I'm just photographing the kids running in the house. Or them jumping off the bouncy house in the backyard. Or Britt (his partner) kissing them. Or if at the school, just documenting the students doing their thing. So those are the moments that are most accessible to me now. I read somewhere that photographers get overwhelmed with trying to find the moment when they are right in the moment and never being able to appreciate that from right where they are.*

—Anyabwile Love in conversation with karim brown,
"Black Folk Just Being: karim brown on the Everyday"

I have been dreading writing this interlude for quite some time. The graceful but persistent text messages of my brother and co-author, Chris, ensuring that I do not chalk this section altogether, are evidence of such. As the mom-moms and aunties would say to a child who is trying their best, "Bless his heart" and his patience. I guess what has had me in a chokehold from writing are my insecurities around being able to produce words that would be worth reading on a page. Often, as a photographer, I have always had my photographs do the heavy "talking" with my audience, which would grant me the ability to play passenger as my wife often does when we go on our elongated family road trips. As I am sure you have heard more than enough times, I grew comfortable with the vexing cliché, "pictures are worth a thousand words." But, as said earlier, my brother would not leave me the hell alone, so here I am now, doing the thing.

It was a convergence of becoming Muslim, my introduction to Black Studies, *The Autobiography of Malcolm X*, my ability to obtain enough bread to own my first camera, the anger espoused by my becoming relatively conscious of my Blackness and its relationship with the greater context of the world that shoved me into using the camera to articulate the contradictions, realties, joy, sorrow, the precarious, and the precocity—what I would consider to be the everyday existence of Black folk. Like a baby who can finally see and begin to understand who mom and dad are, that is how I first engaged with my camera and the art of photography—overwhelmed with contentment and filled with an intense excitement for the possibilities the medium could express. Now, five years into my practice, I, at times, reflect on those early days of becoming a photographer. I was as green as a day in May, a morning during peak harvest season—internalizing my favorite photographers' compositions and rationale for practice, trying to replicate the essence of every frame they ever produced.

Out of the many Black photographers I love and hold dear to my heart, Dawoud Bey's portraiture and visual love letters to 1960s, '70s, and '80s Harlem still deliver a debilitating jab to my spirit. His work lands like Iron Mike's uppercut in the early '90s—glorious (for the observer; devastating for the opponent), intentional, and mind-altering. This deep study of Bey's work inevitably led me to roam the streets of my home—

North Philly and West Philly. However, before holding a camera to the faces of the community, I felt it was important to consider the possible relationships that Black folk had to the medium, especially considering that photographing involves a push-and-pull dynamic, that of relinquishing trust and proving oneself trustworthy. Rightfully so; it is justifiable for Black folks to be skeptical of their image being recorded, because historically the images that have appeared of us in the public media have not been used to propagate our common humanity.

It was obligatory of me to engage with folk in a way that would ensure to them that I intended to keep a balanced record—not of Black excellence nor our downtroddenness—of our daily living practices. Day-to-day work. Ya know—brothas riding dirt bikes, cats on the corners, a mother's love for her baby girl, little brothas squaring up to blow some steam off, and elders seeking stillness in front of the Lord's church. All of these and many other movements that folk engage in are sustenance and remind us that liberation is in the mundane, not the spectacular. My understanding of liberation is inextricably connected to my practice of photography. To photograph Black folk just existing and being is a weapon and a laboratory, because white supremacy only thrives when we are, in fact, not existing and being on our terms. As a Black photographer who comes out of a long genealogy of cultural workers, I constantly deal with the question of: is it enough to draw my camera's attention to the everyday work of—the existing for no other reason than to exist—Black folk, and if so, what is my responsibility to reflecting, recording, and continuing those bitter and sweet moments? All things, both beautiful and ugly, emerge from an imagination. As you engage with this literary and visual meditation, I ask you to do as Meek Mill instructed us in "Blue Notes": "Take a few steps back . . . and look at yourself / Matter fact, take yourself outside your body / And then look at yourself." In other words, remove yourself just enough to immerse yourself in a Black Philly lived experience. The city most certainly needs something, and that need lies right in front of us.

Salaams,
karim brown

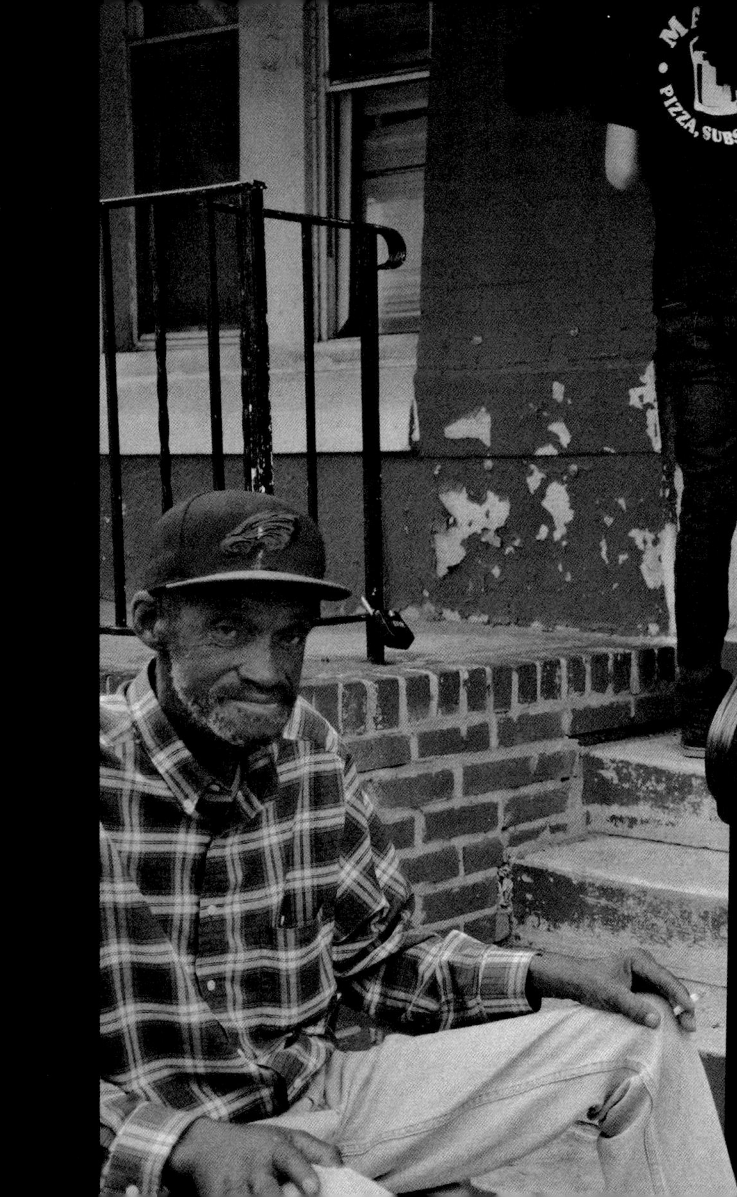
PIZZA, SUBS

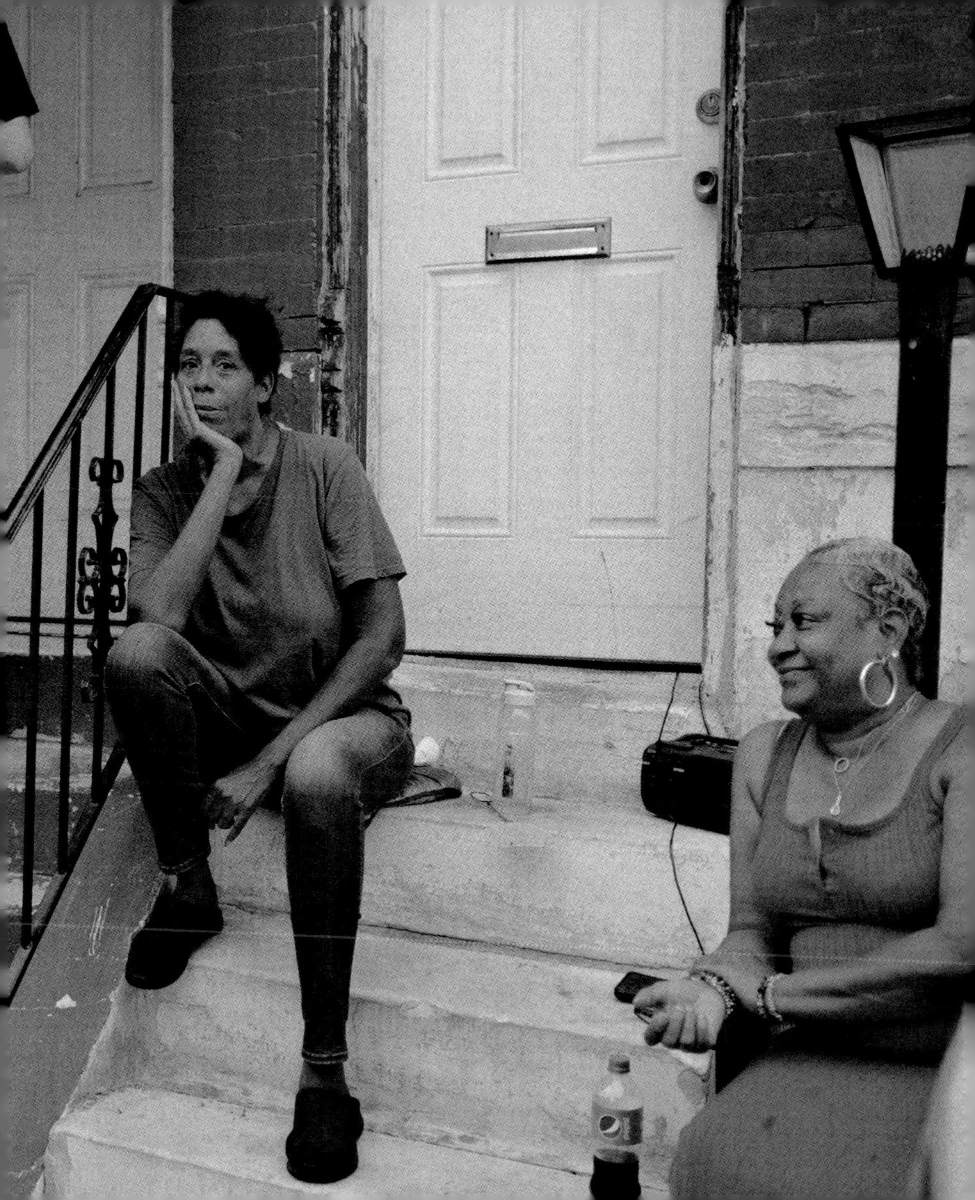

you gotta be outside
(an ode to the poets on the stoop)

There was no way for me to understand it at the time, but the talk that filled the kitchen those afternoons was highly functional. It served as therapy, the cheapest kind available to my mother and her friends. Not only did it help them recover from the long wait on the corner that morning and the bargaining over their labor, it restored them to a sense of themselves and reaffirmed their self-worth. Through language they were able to overcome the humiliations of the workday.

But more than therapy, that freewheeling, wide-ranging, exuberant talk functioned as an outlet for the tremendous creative energy they possessed. They were women in whom the need for self-expression was strong, and since language was the only vehicle readily available to them they made of it an art form that—in keeping with the African tradition in which art and life are one—was an integral part of their lives.

And their talk was a refuge.

—Paule Marshall, "Poets in the Kitchen"

Rock, you probably thinking where I be getting all this stuff from, but I'm telling you, it all came and comes from being outside. And listening, like really listening, on the inside too. Like in that dangerous childlike way you would get an ass-whooping for, just because you loved information, loved illegitimate access to knowledge you wasn't supposed to have, especially when it's considered dangerous in the wrong hands.

Yeah, that was me, bro. At Sunday family dinner over at my aunt's house on Chester's West End, pretending to be watching *Fresh Prince* reruns, but really sitting there eavesdropping on grown folk business happening around the bend of the smells wafting in from the kitchen. You know, we was never allowed in the kitchen if it wasn't time to eat, but if you sat right near the part of my Aunt Allora's living room by the TV that was next to the bathroom that opened the other way into the kitchen, you could hear it *all.* All that stuff they said you wasn't supposed to know.

At times, it was a collective affair, navigating the puzzle of what I heard my friend Destiny call "the secret Black maternal arts of concealment." Me and my siblings trying to figure out why we can't sleep over at our cousin's house this weekend. Why the one time my pops who promised he was coming to get us to go to the Chuck E. Cheese on Baltimore Pike never got back to our messages left on his pager. Like all of it. What Mom's doctor actually said to her about her recurrent cancer diagnosis. You know, all those things beyond a Black babychild's place.

But me, myself? I was early like Freeway. I knew I was good at spelling because when my aunts and 'em would switch into that ol' spelling bee act to get over on a revealing part of the story, not knowing they really wasn't fooling nobody. I could've been the CUSD [Chester Upland School District] spelling bee champ. I was putting the pieces together. I spent many winters incubating a deciphering practice all my own.

But there was always my fatal flaw, my Achilles heel: not knowing how to keep my mouth shut with all that counterintelligence I was gathering.

Rock, your boy was a leaky faucet.

It would all just spill out of me, right at the wrong time, in the earshot of too many traitorous codefendants. And then, quick and in a flash, a gasp became the grounds for swift admonishment, with Moms finishing the proceedings with a stern, "You need to learn to think before you speak."

I never understood as a Black babychild all what that African proverb intended I recognize. I mean, I get it meant in Black-mama-talk that you working my last nerve so don't give me a reason to take it up a notch . . . but like I'm saying what it really, really meant. The response I would often mumble out the hushed side of my mouth, so clear to me today that I can still recite:

> But sometimes I gotta say what I think so I can think about what I just said. How else you suppose to know what you saying all before the fact of saying it?

I had to get it out. Something like these stories, Rock. I had to let loose or lose some inside part of me in the process.

Since my mother's untimely transition, which is way too close and too bound up with this memory, I dream she may one day find my adolescent truths a reason to laugh. *Oh, to hear her laugh again, Rock.*

My blueprint to dangerously spy in the enemy country's listening being and becoming a gift and a curse. What my momma loved, wanted, and needed me to learn was cultivating discernment, but discernment is hard to earn for Black boys taking in grown Black folk business amid a very noisy, harsh, and unfair city. Like Martin King once said, "I was always on the verge of being mesmerized by uncertainty," so I'd just speak, Rock, forgetting that other part he said about the calling to speak often being a vocation of agony.

But, Rock, now I can take in all the grown-folk business I want. And I'm telling you fam, if we looking to realize an alternative arrangement of this place, we going to be needing to get comfortable with listening. We gon' have to be outside, make a little spot on the stoop. Bring the radio; gotta have the Black radio. WDAS [105.3 FM] if you plan on talking with the elders.

And we need folk to go tell it on the mountains. We gon' need everybody heard. We all be knowing the secrets to survival. It's in the letting loose; it's in the telling.

If you outside, there's something that happens in those chaotic *gumbo ya-ya* stoop-circle conversations that bring us into community. Yeah, that's the way of saying it; before you buss it up with folks for hours on the stoop, they might be your neighbors, but you can't call them your community.

I mean, if you don't know them at all, like they don't never make themselves available, Ms. Frances said they ain't nothing but new tenants, and the privileged ones, homeowners. She's serious about this. If you move to a block in Philadelphia, you need to get to know your neighbors. She said you don't know somebody until you know their grandma's story. You have to earn your right to belong; it's an active responsibility.

Ms. Frances say people too easily forget or ignore that come hell or high water, you gon' have to rely on community someday to save your ass. Ain't no reason why we shouldn't know when the next block clean-up is. Audre Lorde says, "Without community, there is no liberation," but in Philadelphia, without community, you might as well cancel Christmas, at least all them package deliveries you thought was gonna be there by the time you got home. They steal dishes out your kitchen 'round here.

But, Rock, the other part of listening with folk, with Us, is that it's not staged, it's not a performance, it's most often sincere, not verifiably honest the whole time, but always sincere. And the marvelous beauty of sincerity, of folk making it plain, of folk exaggerating the facts to tell new truths, of folk disclosing a whole 'nother story just by being silent at the wrong time, of folk having just the right timely ad-lib, of folk walking away for a moment because the laughter is too much to hold in their insides. It's truly "*Nothing Like It.*" It all *feels* like music, like our true Black blues. It all feels like Us.

Rock, Amiri Baraka said we got to be outside to keep our "*omm bomm ba boom*" alive.

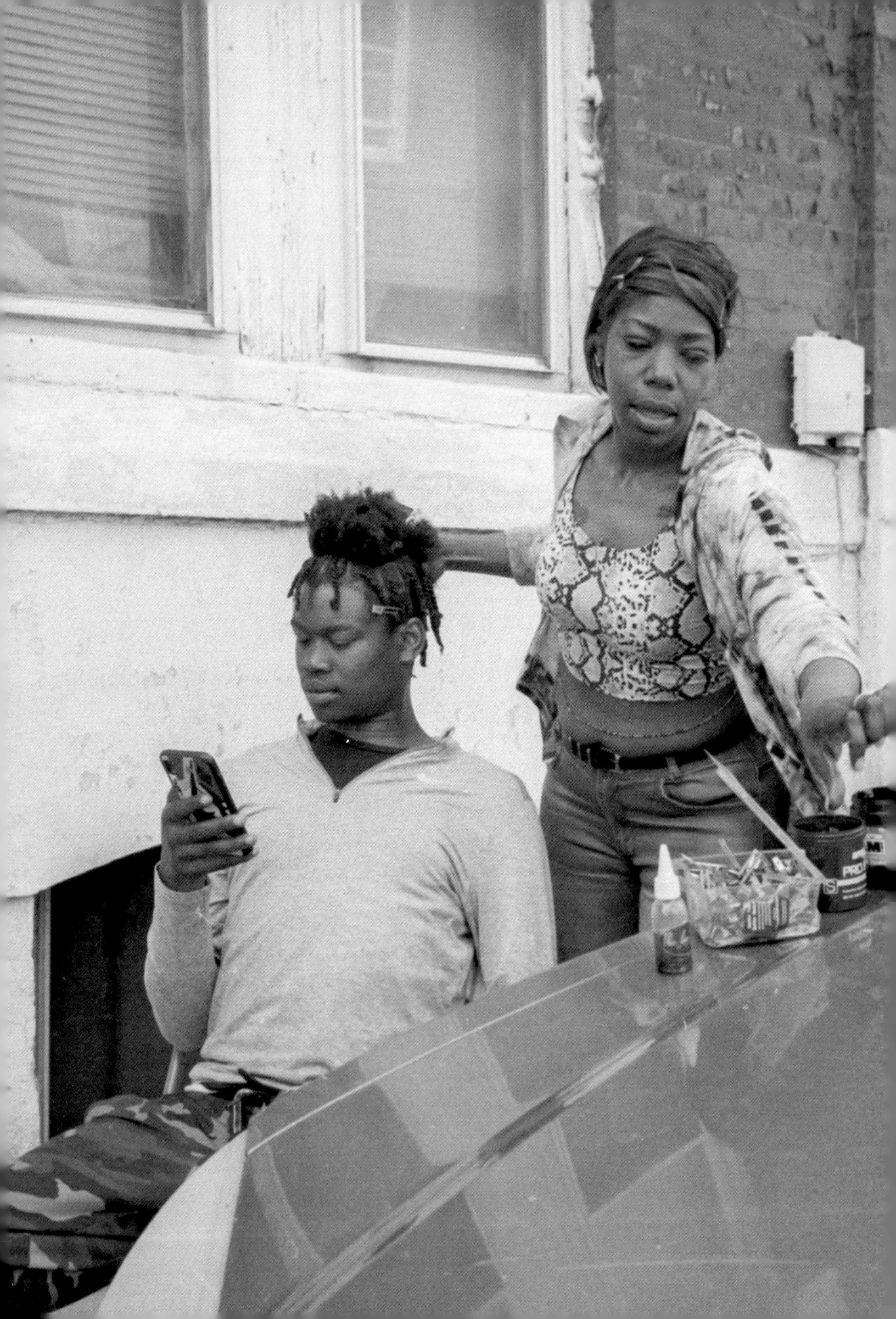

As Baraka say, 'The duty of a poet is to say as exactly as possible what it is he or she means.' Because what you're dealing with is so intangible. It's why we have to speak in similes and parables and metaphors. You can't speak in the language of the technocrat. And I think my primary duty is to stay in touch with myself and be as true as I possibly can in examining myself, and to communicate that to other people and to let them know that I am essentially a good human being and that they are too. And that's what communication is. I've had some readings that—and you can tell when a good reading go down, because people start talking to each other, they'll start touching. That's the art. That's when the art happens. The art happens when the poet and the poem and the people are in communion. It's communication happening. Art doesn't happen in a book. Or a picture hanging on that wall. You know, it takes people.

—Etheridge Knight, "A MELUS Interview: Etheridge Knight"

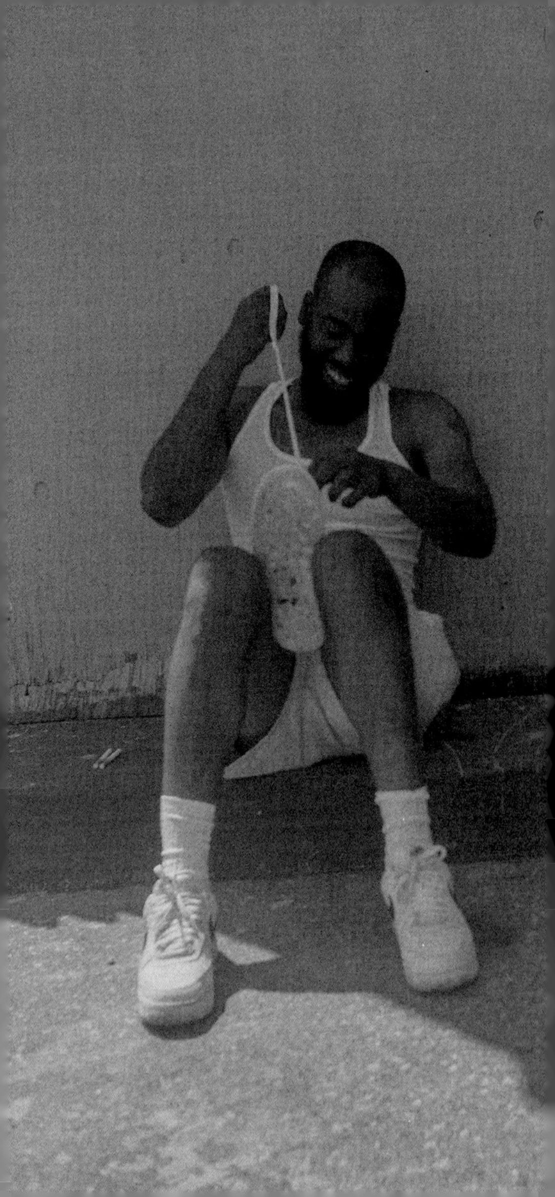

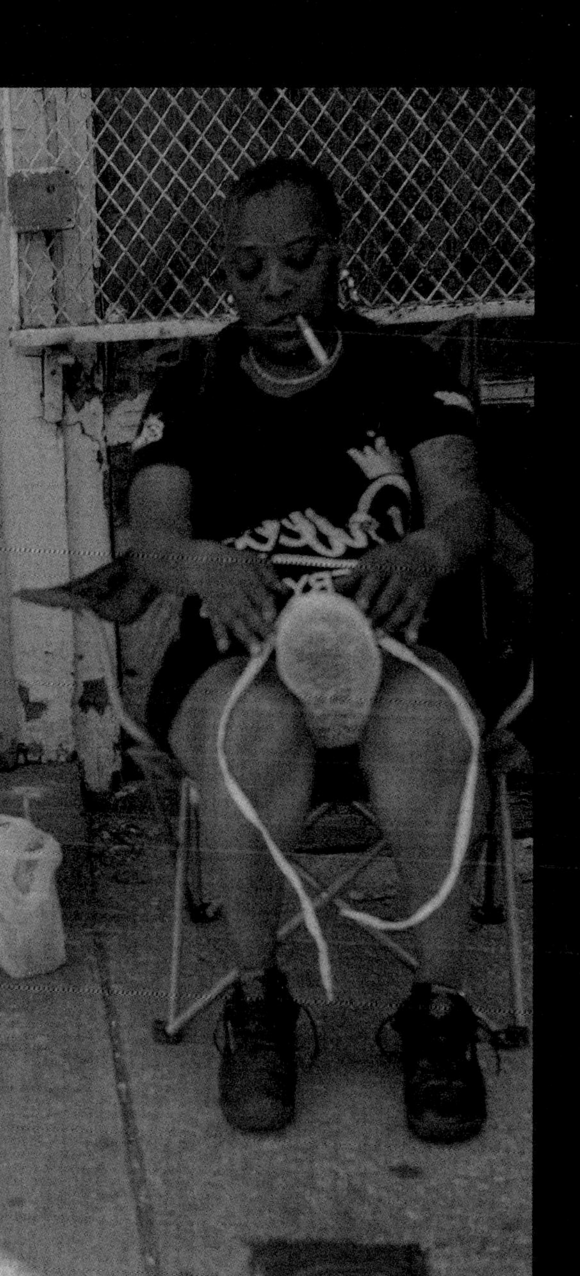

stay ready so you don’t have to get ready

Staying ready isn’t just for the tough times, it’s also being prepared to accept the blessings.

—Tamara Nopper

Revolution begins with the self, in the self.

—Toni Cade Bambara, *The Black Woman: An Anthology*

Rock, I'm talking about preparation. I'm talking about being prepared to receive an answer, some *what is to be done* and actively experiment with it. Like really tarry and struggle with it. More specifically, Rock, I'm talking about what the jazz legend Henry Threadgill was talking about. Hear me out for a minute:

> INTERVIEWER: Now so much of—because everybody in the group is an improviser and improvisation requires being in the moment.
>
> THREADGILL: Yeah . . .
>
> INTERVIEWER: Is there a way that you prepare to be in the moment? How do you train yourself to be in the moment?
>
> THREADGILL: You don't. You just, you just, you just prepare. But you know, it's going to be a surprise. You don't control the factors. It's like the rain. You can't get ready for the rain.
>
> INTERVIEWER: You can have an umbrella.
>
> THREADGILL: You're going to get wet. It's okay. Umbrella or no umbrella, you're going to get wet. You can't prepare for the rain.
>
> INTERVIEWER: Do you get wet on stage?
>
> THREADGILL: Yes. Yeah. It's nice.

Stop laughing, bro. I'm serious.

> THREADGILL: Yeah. What we do is, the process that I'm involved in with the musicians is everything. It is the thing that enables us to handle what happens in the moment. It's a process that I had learned over the years how to work on music, and I can't think of the German word, but I use the German word for *rehearse*. It doesn't mean rehearse. What it means is to explore and search. The American word "rehearse" is just about going in, read the text from left to right. If you read the text from left to right, you get it correct, you're finished. There's nothing else to do.
>
> We read the text from left to right, right to left, tear the whole text down, reinvent it every possible way that we can imagine, drop out parts of the text, never add anything to the text but completely destroy the text, re-invent the text over and over, leave out parts of the text, then we know something about what we're about to do.

INTERVIEWER: You do that strictly in the exploring . . .

THREADGILL: Yes.

INTERVIEWER: . . . phase?

THREADGILL: Yeah.

INTERVIEWER: Or do you do that at the performance?

THREADGILL: No.

I've been sitting with this for a minute. This orientation to process, the tides, currents, and waves of it all, the probing of it all.

Rock, we gotta know that whatever is coming, whatever is around the corner for us, we still gon' get wet anyway. That shouldn't stop a damn thing tho' if we committed to searching for new ground. We must still commit to an expansive process of figuring out what we all about to do regardless.

You better dedicate yourself to that woodshedding of the exploring phase. We got to have higher goals for ourselves and our people. We got to be planning on moving on up. Best be prepared for what's about to go down. We got to plan to work, study, create, and build. But know, in all the ways, we still gonna be getting wet. It's inherent to the practice of striving. And it might not feel nice. But I'd rather be wet on the move than be drenched and shamed and stuck in the mud.

If we stay ready, we don't have to get ready. What does it mean to get ourselves ready for Black liberation? Where's our printed schedule of those necessary community rehearsals for living sovereign?

It's true Rock, that me and too many of our bros shoot ourselves in the foot by focusing too much on the necessity of armed struggle rather than the urgency of the inner struggle. Those stray bullets from untended triggers can kill Us too.

Did they hear Lauryn Hill when she said, "How you gonna win when you ain't right within?" Yeah, she may come late every now and then, but them words was right on time. We got to focus on our insides more, like our down-South cousin Kiese [Laymon] be saying.

Like Rock, I remember this incredible interview with Paula Moya and Junot Díaz where he says:

> *Most importantly these [women-of-color feminist] sisters offered strategies of hope, spinning the threads that will make escape from this labyrinth possible. It wasn't an easy thread to seize—this movement towards liberation required the kind of internal bearing witness of our own role in the social hell of our world that most people would rather not engage in. It was a tough praxis, but a potentially earth-shaking one too. Because rather than strike at this issue or that issue, this internal bearing of witness raised the possibility of denying our oppressive regimes the true source of their powers—which is, of course,* our *consent,* our *participation. This kind of praxis doesn't attack the head of the beast, which will only grow back; it strikes directly at the beast's heart, which we nurture and keep safe in our own.*
>
> —Junot Díaz, "The Search for Decolonial Love: A Conversation between Junot Díaz and Paula M. L. Moya"

Yeah, it's ironic because not too long after reading this, a couple women of color 'round here alleged brother Junot was too committed to being a fiction writer in his real life.

I mean, Rock, it's hard work to live well; you had your documented struggles too. Mine as well. We still gotta measure Us right tho; there's always something left to love.

I honor Brother Junot on this front: transnational women-of-color feminisms are incredibly necessary for shaping our city's future, if we are trying to have a worthy one beyond this "*changing same*." And I mean that in a way that allows space for not all women-of-color feminisms always all the time either. It's not simply an identity thing. It's a knowledge thing. I know that your, and our, only chance at full liberation is inextricably intertwined with theirs. So, like Junot once said, we better duck these arrows aimed at our heart, because they certainly gon' keep coming until we get right.

And Rock, if my songs are me first, then I must recognize I too am still forever working on it, that heavy business of becoming whole and well. So, I can't point the finger at Brother Junot without holding that I could find a way to sit together and figure out how we might both plan to own up to all of the past versions of ourselves. We must keep in touch with the past versions of ourselves. We can't heal without it. I'll save that for another time tho, not for this conversation between Us, Rock.

Rock, there's some working answers here about what we can do about the city which again, Toni Cade Bambara said, "begins with the self, in the self." A friend of hers, June Jordan, got something for us too. You an artist, right?

> *I'm not afraid of knowing anything. An artist can't afford to pretend that her accomplishment derives from an unconscious spontaneous happenstance because that's not true. We're talking about discipline, a knowledge that is very complicated and that deserves all the serious, self-conscious commitment that any high calling requires. What I mean by high calling is that it's not immediately obvious. The usefulness of it may not be always immediately obvious. It's like faith. Love is a high calling to me. It's not about usefulness. It's just there, but you really care about it more than you care about anything else.*
>
> —June Jordan, "Creation is Revolutionary"

She knows this: for Us to reach our higher goals, we got to have a higher calling we got to be preparing for. We must begin within and we can't be afraid of no self-discipline. We can't be afraid of rigor. Of investigating our faults. Of our failures to receive and provide good love. Of figuring out our patterns of evasions and excuses and flat-out lies. It's the artist's struggle, yeah, but something is coming back to me, what's that thing James Baldwin said? I feel like it has usefulness here:

> *It seems to me that the artist's struggle for his integrity must be considered as a kind of metaphor for the struggle, which is universal and daily, of all human beings on the face of this globe to get to become human beings.*

We have to prepare ourselves to be the answer. It's up to all of us if we trying to achieve something different for the city, Rock. Facts.

But hold up.

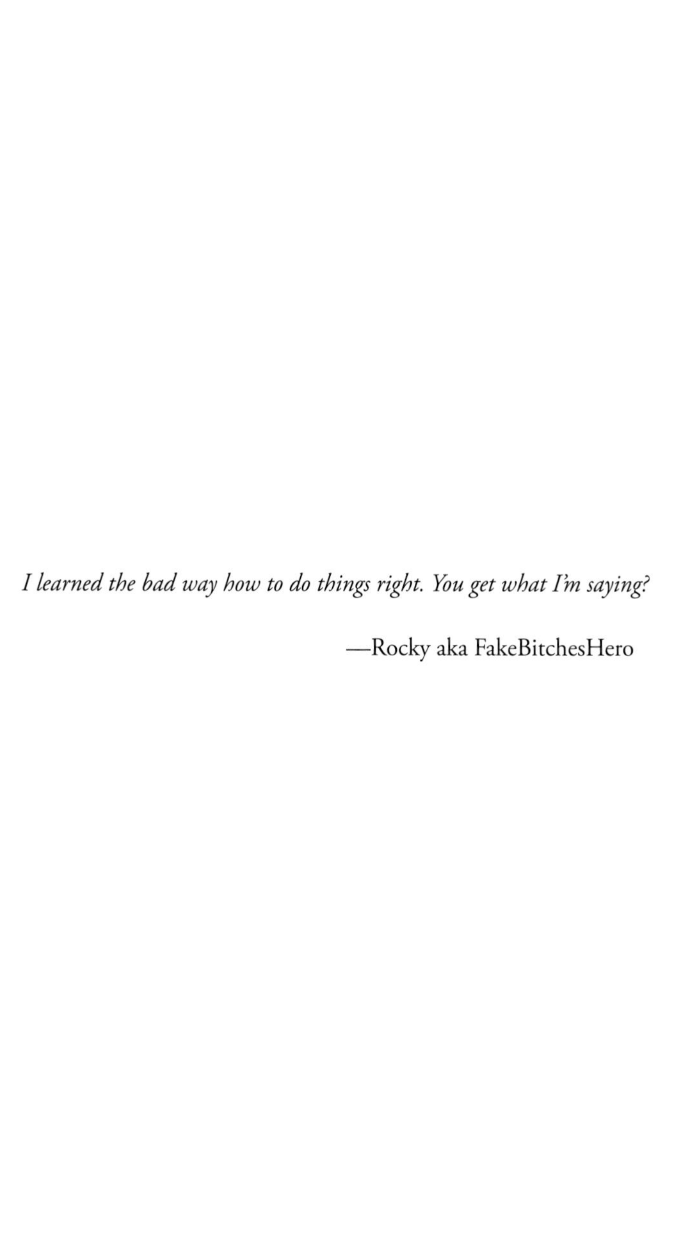

I learned the bad way how to do things right. You get what I'm saying?

—Rocky aka FakeBitchesHero

It's difficult to do this chapter in full character because it's too often true that many of Us are character acting. I'd like to take a moment to thank many of the Black queer feminist friends that took a chance over the years on once trying to tell me truths that incited the efforts of self-work necessary to produce whatever I write next. I already know it won't live up to the full truths of what y'all all the way meant. Keep the bar low. I hope my striving philosophy helps here. I wanna be better, and even sometimes not simply for y'all, but for the sake of myself and our shared future.

I also thought through the whole thing of whether I needed, as a matter of public penance, to replay and explore some moment I may have failed one of Us to show that I'm not easily contained in that prison of being perceived as one of the good ones. I've erred before, and not always with a chance to confront and care for who and what those failings inspired. And I certainly remain capable of doing so again, and I hope y'all know that about yourself too. However, for the purposes of this fiction, I decided it was more important I face up to my own personal failings and what's still killing Us in my real life. These things deserve true multidimensional human processes and not flattened into the pages of a self-produced print product.

Rock, I'll be honest. I only learned most of these things last year. I got a sense of the general principles, but I'm still failing forward all the time. The general idea, which I think comes from bell hooks, is: cisheteropatriarchy begins with our own self-harm and hurt people harm people everyday, b.

"Cisheteropatriarchy" just being a very long word for describing how our brothers and 'em be struggling with love's address. Simply, a long word for when love don't live here no more. A reminder that we lost something along the way, sometimes never thinking we had something to begin with. Love, a gift, worth treasuring. The hook being that it's really all about love. That's the gift we have the opportunity to give ourselves, every day. And can't nobody take that away.

As Black men, it's obviously true that we're misshaped by violent logics that we inherited out of another peoples' violent-ass imagination. It's a truth. Not the whole truth. But a real one.

Yet, if we are to become honorable, to become human in the way Sylvia Wynter and Suzanne Cesaire teach us, that must eventually come to mean that we got to commit to refuse to reproduce those violent logics of misogyny, of queer antagonism, of transphobia, etc. Not solely for those folks' sake either, but our own way of learning how to responsibly stand upright and return to the source. The source of our power. The source of our healing. The source of our renewal. The source of our liberation.

It's got to be something worthwhile to hold on to knowing that you can choose, better yet knowing you already chose, to love somebody. You see I didn't say "try" there. To have loved and lost is better than losing love. The gift is in the giving. Another Toni Morrison mic drop.

We got to be practicing love and repair so much so that we get real good at it and muster a way to share those secret recipes with someone else. That gotta do something for the souls of Black folk in this life and possibly others too. I've not arrived all the way there yet, to the point that such a practice feels easy. I'm starting to realize that just might be the point.

Love's uncertainty keeps you awake on the road, in the woodshed, in its exploring phase. Falling. Rising. Courageously contemplating the sorts of ideas about how to treat folks in ways that do more than counter violence but actively witness all the beauty and dignity present in our just being-with and existing-with. Unlearning everything else that stands against it. This must be where Jordan's serious self-conscious commitment comes calling.

What strategies, what language do we have, to explore our innermost worlds? Do we invest the intimate time necessary to sit with our own unanswered questions? What sorts of questions do we Black men make up that need answering and what sort of answers do we Black men give that need questioning?

Rock, I'm not saying you wasn't being genuine when you asked what the city needed and didn't know. I feel you. I believe you. We far too often don't know. It's been suppressed and hidden, but we can recover it. We must. I'm just saying I might've just learned last year that it can't be Black women and femmes' job to provide those answers for Us. This one can't be on them too.

We got to reach deep within on our own for that higher calling, those higher goals. We got to stop performing the act, stay with the trouble of our lives, and be prepared to get wet. We ain't gonna get Us free without getting wet.

Pause.

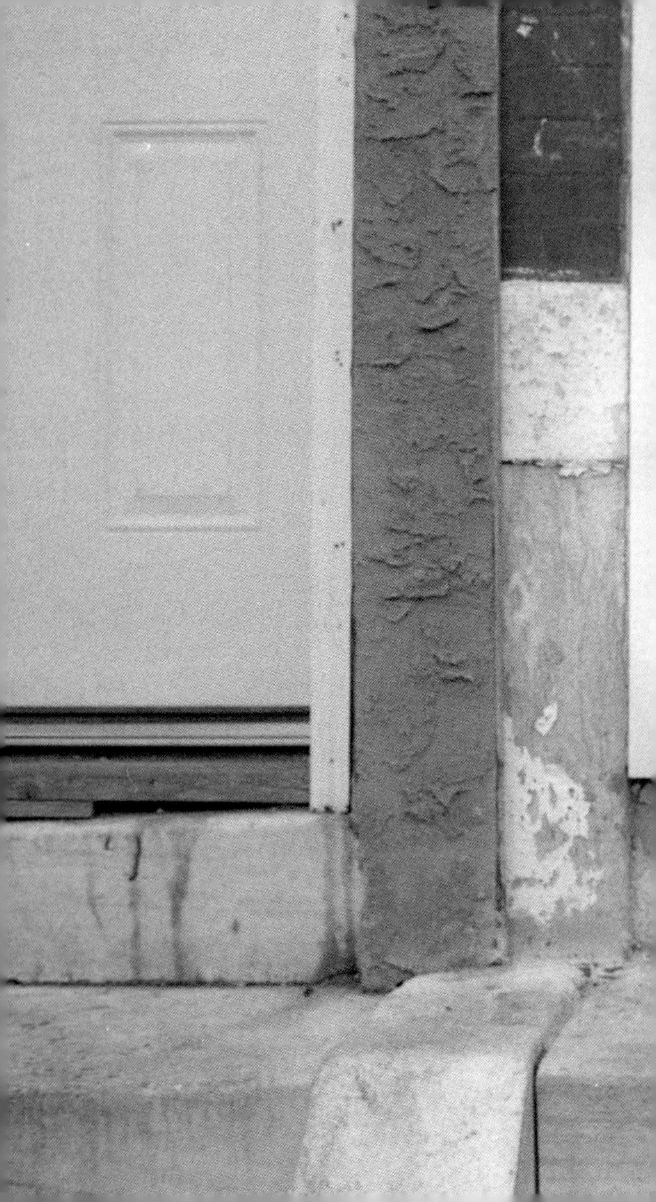

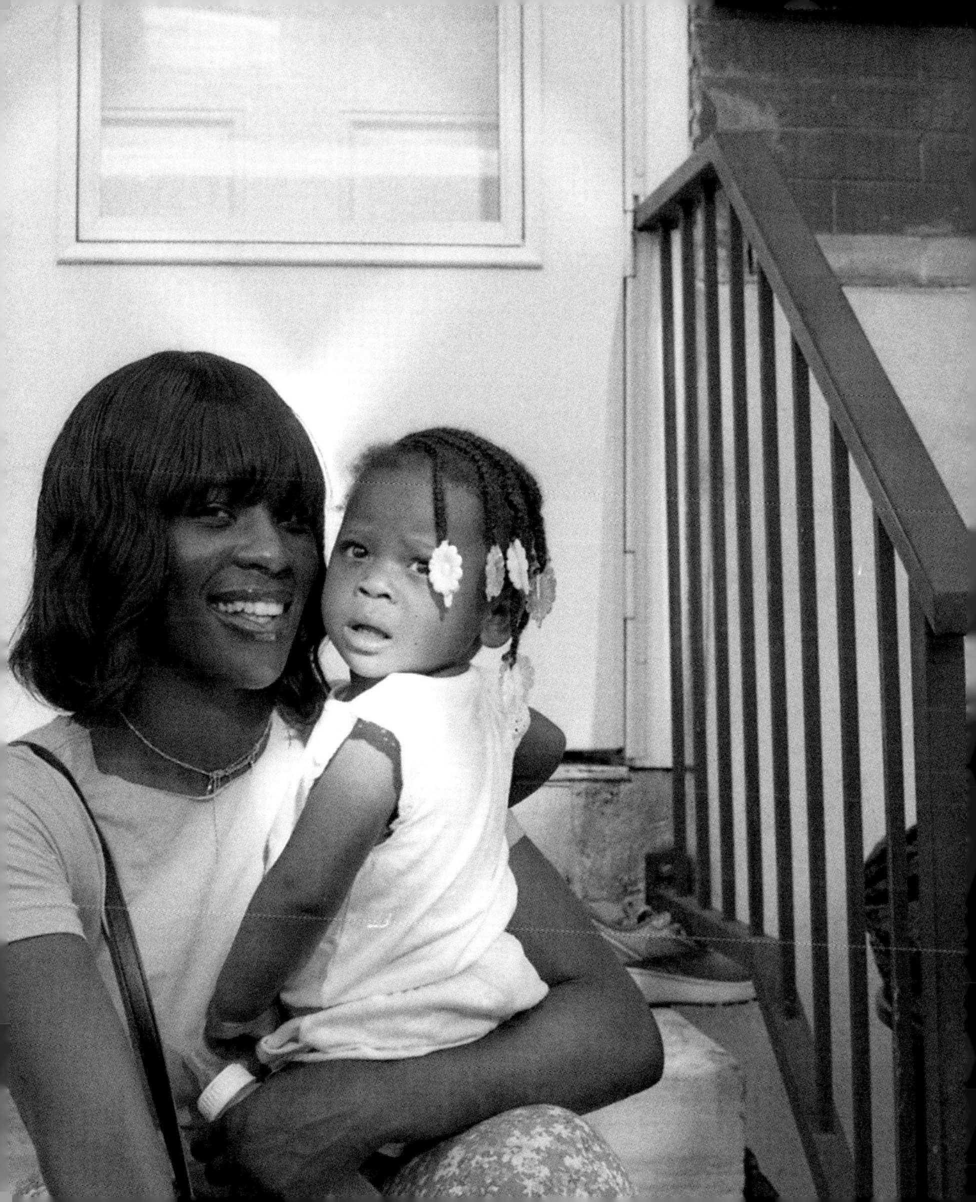

all about the love

When gratitude is present, ain't no way that I could stay the same.

—Navy Blue, "Phases"

Rock, is it too early or too cliché or too vague or too repetitive to say that Black love may be the strongest working answer we got? Not because it's gonna get Us to this mythical destination of forever-lasting Black liberation we been talking about any sooner—I mean not without any of us embracing some super, heavy-duty, urgent, collective, make me over soul-work. Still tho, even then, no guarantees.

But getting all up close and intimate with Black love does reveal the possibility that when we do get there to that thin but kinda sturdy foothold of Black liberation, we might not immediately collapse under the weight, the tonnage of our unaddressed wounds. Yeah, I believe we can heal if we keep the main thing the main thing like Jalen Hurts be saying.

We gotta be doing away with the illusions, emptying out the baggage of our long lives, getting to the nitty-gritty in service of nurturing another Black life into the fullness of their fragile and interdependent freedom. We gotta be learning to rise up and really love somebody.

We might wanna first begin with practice learning how to love our deepest, darkest, primitive afrikan selves. The self that is still rooted in a homeplace white folk can't conquer nor exhaust. We may only then struggle to figure out how to keep the same energy with someone new. That got to be evidence of something city-altering and needs-answering that we can claim for this experiment. This hypothesis of that different thing out there we been searching for. That thing I've been telling you I kinda know already exists somewhere in and around here. We really got to sit with this Black love thing some more. Rock, remember how I said Toni Morrison is always important?

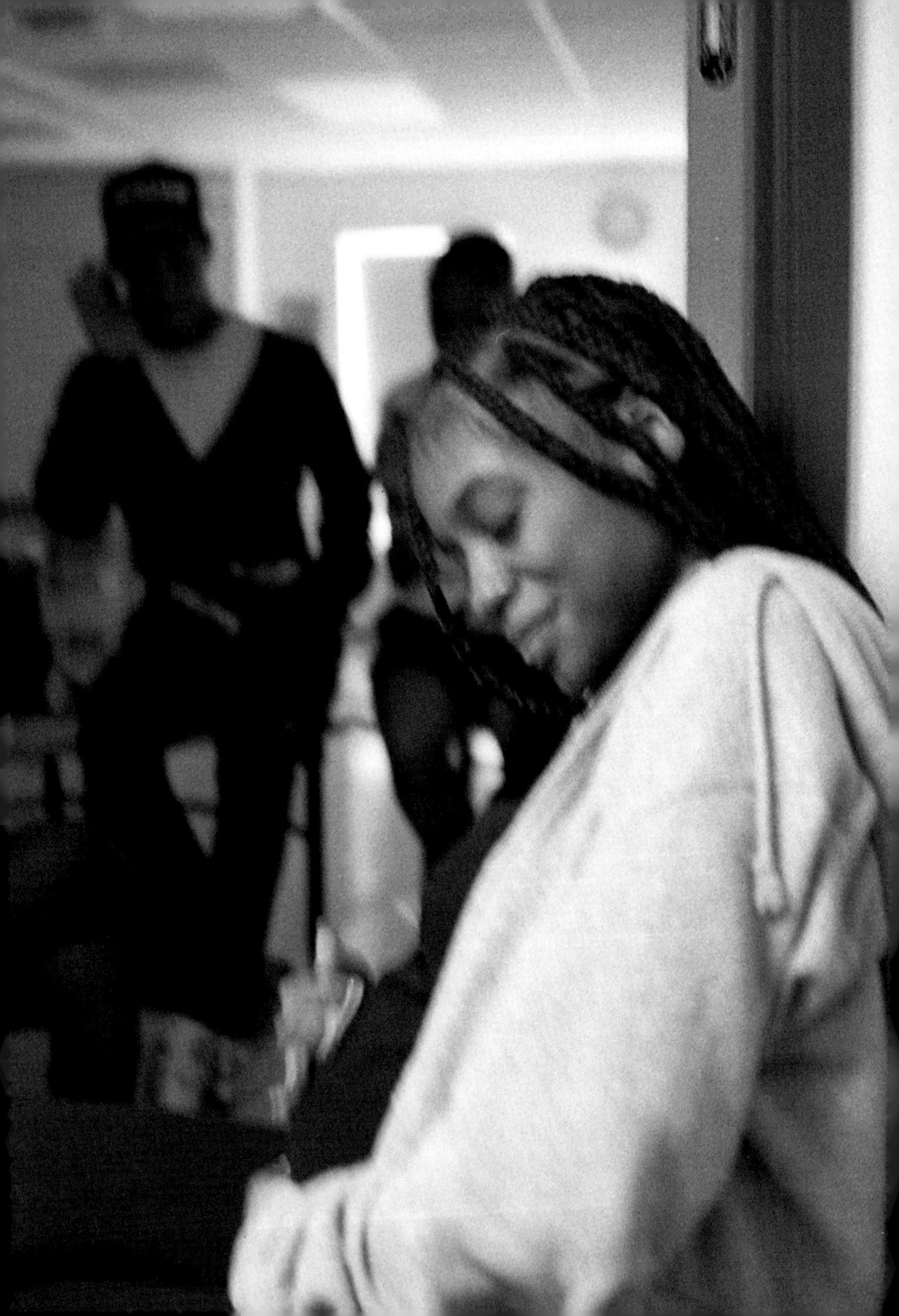

MOYERS: You say love is a metaphor, and when I go back through the novels, love is there in so many different ways and forms that—and particularly when I look at the women in your novels, at the extraordinary things they do for love. There's the grandmother who has her leg amputated so that she can have an insurance policy that will buy a house and take care of her children as they grow up. There's Sethe, who is willing to kill her children before the slave catchers can come and seize them. What kind of love is that?

MORRISON: Some of it's very fierce. Powerful. Distorted, even, because the duress they work under is so overwhelming. But I think they believed, as I do, while it may be true that, you know, people say, "I didn't ask to be born," I think we did, and that's why we're here. We are here, and we have to do something nurturing that we respect before we go. We must. It is more interesting, more complicated, more intellectually demanding and more morally demanding to love somebody, to take care of somebody, to make one other person feel good. Now the dangers of that are the dangers of setting oneself up as a martyr or as, you know, the one without whom it would not be done.

MOYERS: Paul D says to Sethe, "Your love is too thick." Is that what you're talking about here?

MORRISON: Too thick. That's right. It can get to be very excessive.

MOYERS: And how do we know when a love is too thick?

MORRISON: We don't, we really don't. That's a big problem. We don't know when to stop, as Baby Suggs says, "When is it too much and when is it not enough?" That is the problem of the human mind and the soul. But we have to try that. We have to try that. We have to do that. And not doing it is so poor for the self. It's so poor for the mind. It's so uninteresting to live without that, and it has no risk. There's no risk involved. And that just seems to make life not just livable, but a gallant, gallant event.

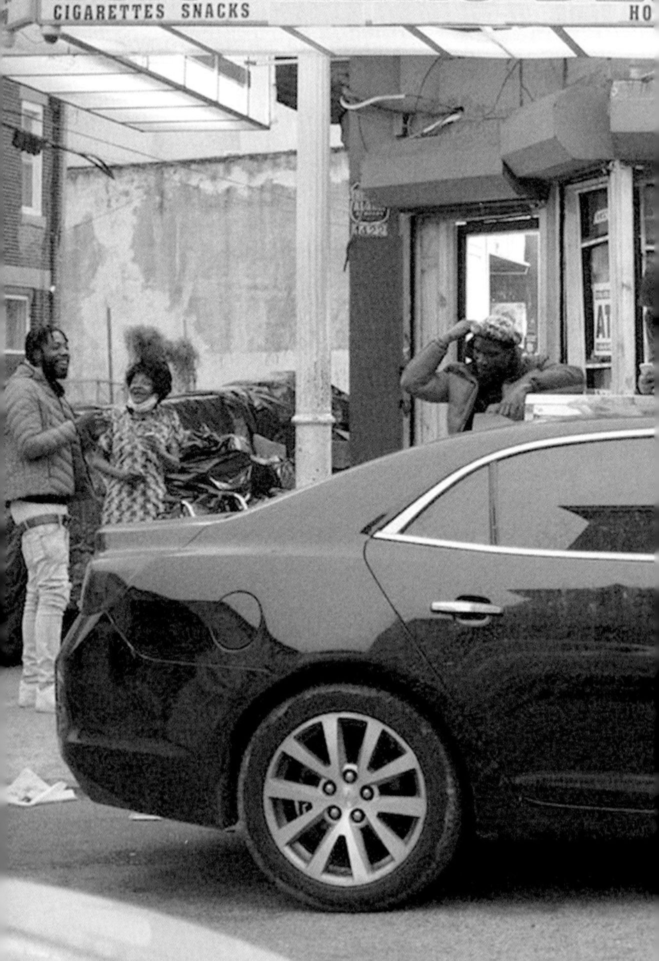
BROTHERS DE
CIGARETTES SNACKS

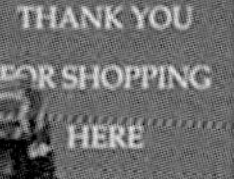
THANK YOU
FOR SHOPPING
HERE
BUSINESS

groundings with my brothers

If I had one wish, I'd free the homies.

—Vince Staples, "AYE! FREE THE HOMIES"

Rock, I got into a Facebook debate years ago with a brother, a friend of a friend who gon' say that our mutual brother, fresh off a major life achievement, came from *nothing*. Who and where is nothing?

Like I ain't meet this brother outside in my city and talked with his mom and his peoples and know what Chester church and community programs he was raised in. Killed me upon reading that. It's possible I had been drinking that day; I'm definitely known to impulsively overshare online once buzzed but let's be real. That's grounds for a comment. OK, maybe I should have DM-ed.

But it hit me, because I'm weary that too many of us really be out here saying, believing, misunderstanding, and spreading lies that we came from *nothing*. Like we haven't been sent forward in this upside-down world with a duty given to us by our ancestors to make things right. Like we don't have a responsibility to acknowledge and add into the collective pool of Black genius, the accumulating collective intelligence of our historical struggle, distilled from our daily encounters and squabbles that inform and incubate epic resistance movements. We come from something to hold on to.

You gotta hear me on this one, Rock. The lie that *we* came from nothing is that same sort of "all what we all pretending to not know" that holds us back from realizing we are the decisive force in the transformation of the city. Nah, fam. We ain't Sidney Poitier nor Walter Lee Younger, so we got to drop the act. We really holding on to something, something so powerful inside when we measuring it right.

It's not my purpose to fully explain the shape of the feeling and its flight in our lives, just to suggest to us all that it is there. That we can reach for it in our moments of strife. What if we were to live our lives not demanding we wish upon a star of some illusory concept of "making it *out*," crossing that chasm from our nothingness into being somebody, never realizing who, what, and why we already be. What if by mere birthright, we claimed our victory knowing our crown has already been bought and paid for?

We got truths and reasons for our becoming. I don't got all the words, but I intend to live my life knowing it's something there. Like it's in my possession. I intend to live my life knowing someone loved me, somebody loves us, that someone prepped the ground for us to be a force of Black personhood and we owe it to them to not be pretending we were never called into this beautiful, inexhaustive, worldmaking inheritance. I intend to live my life taking the leap of faith on loving Us.

Hard to explain in a public Facebook comment, I suppose. Yet, when we stop, look, and listen, we can feel its presence. Reminds me of this time I was at the barbershop back in the day.

Rock, I use to spend whole days at the barbershop. Partly because it's a place of refuge as a Black man growing up in the city daily slaying the dragons of the white man's world in order to bring home a check. Partly because there is nothing more entertaining than sharing memories from way back when, only interrupted by debates over the *who-did-it-betters*, whether that be Kobe or Lebron, *Goodfellas* or *Casino*, Janet or Sade, Jay or Nas.

But practically, the most telling part is because my cousin/play-brother is my barber and has been since I've been fifteen. The family/business line been incredibly blurry since the first time I would trade my Nissan's weekend gas tank to him for a haircut. If I was to head to the barbershop at 2:00 p.m., I probably wouldn't get home until midnight. Sometimes 2:00 a.m. before a hood holiday (e.g., a warm weather Saturday). Yes, folks would park 'round the Gold Room, get a cut, and head in to flex.

One summer weekday, we sat together (I sat, he worked at his own slow-but-steady pace) while I was on my flex time from managing summer youth programming at the nearby community center. A young Puerto Rican brother, couldn't have been no more than fifteen, came to sit down in one of the chairs near the constant-leftover-platter-occupied microwave. He sat down, tightly holding a folded piece of paper in his adolescent hands, and no doubt seemed pretty somber for the summertime freedom we all expected he enjoyed. *Rock, remember life before you had working papers?*

"What's up with you?" My cousin acknowledged his presence, greeting him in the midst of shaping the sideburns of his current client.

"Oh, I ain't here for a haircut, I'm trying to get a tattoo," he said, holding his head up.

Yeah, Rock, forgot to mention, at the time there was a tattoo parlor operating out of the back end of the barbershop, like between where we sat and the bathrooms at the back of the joint. I mean, the brother ran a pretty clean operation and the foot traffic from the barbershop probably helps to build clientele. Black barbershops always gonna be Black men's subterranean marketplace. That's our tradition.

My cousin hit back, "Word. He back there with somebody right now. Should be out in a minute. What you tryna get?" My cousin, and me too from the cheap seats, eyeing the folded-up piece of paper in his hand.

"Let me check it out," as his hand extended to look at the artwork that the young Boricua brought with him. I'm trying to eyeball it from my seat. I'm kinda hesitant and frankly a bit judgmental, watching a young man jumping into what seemed to me to be his first tattoo all willy-nilly.

My mom, rest in power, woulda had some words. It was taught to me while I squirmed in church pews that God cosigned that tattoos were sins against God's temple. If I can see beyond that now, I still have remained tattoo-free, better just in case my time to meet Him comes unexpectedly.

My cousin opened the paper, gave it a quick look-see, shared the youngin' an affirming, heartful nod, and told him it was cool. He took a solemn breath, and kept the convo going, "Who's that?"

"My brother. Did you see the paper the other day?"

"You talking about that thing that happened over the East Side?"

"Yeah, that was my older brother."

Damn, Rock, that hurt me. Because I knew exactly who he meant, and what tragic fate that his older brother faced, over what was ultimately nothing in the grand scheme of everyday offenses. But you know how it goes, anything can become something when we ourselves mischaracterize our precious, beloved lives as nothing to lose.

Rock, sitting there quiet the entire time, I now moved from just not speaking into silent inner reflection, harboring the inside guilt of my jump to judgment that preceded the sincere heartache.

He can't be no more than fifteen.

Still, that hand-drawn artwork was made with all intention of coming to the local barbershop/unlicensed tattoo parlor to get this self-fashioned pencil portrait he conjured from sitting with his fresh grief inked eternally onto his adolescent flesh.

This was his sincere, self-determined, affordable eternal revival service for his brother not more than a week after he had left his side, at least on this hellish earthly physical plane. Here's a young man's heartfelt communion to inscribe and blood-bond his brother's life into his own. A longing to always remember what his brother had meant to him, apparent anytime he looked in the mirror.

A yearning that he, younger brother, still maintained the power to take his older brother everywhere he might have went and would go, even if it that journey was just back home to the East Side. To the courts off Upland Street. To Boots and Bonnets. To Chester High Homecoming. You know, Rock, we Chester folk never leave.

He left his home that morning, committed not to walk another day on this earth without his brother, determined to live for him, provide him a second chance to glimpse new horizons. His brother's life lived through his own.

Rock, he couldn't have been no more than fifteen.

I sat there, now as somber as he was, yet feeling myself over time easing into a silver-lined smile. If only in what may have been his worst of times, I was awarded the opportunity through this young brother's tarrying with impossible feelings to witness love-in-action, alive, and to be written in the flesh in the storage closet of an old dentist office now turned Black barbershop and Black man waiting room and underground tattoo parlor.

Rock, blue moments like that renew my faith that we inherit, through whatever come what may, the intimate sufficiencies to answer the unfair questions of our lives with dignity, grace, and gritty resolve. That young man reminded me that day: our chosen, found, and lost brothers be loved and we must refuse to let our loved ones be framed as if our love, the love of our mothers, the love of our ancestors, ain't already there to invent and carry us as somebody on our own terms. We always already somebody to one of Us. In our blood re-memory too. All I'm saying . . .

And yeah, I should probably stop drinking and opening social media apps. Never ends well.

I'm fortified by long listening sessions with the sanctified music of John Coltrane. Trane: another celestial genius whose sacred voice gives me hope. And by hope I mean blues-inflicted hope that is morally sound; hope learned and earned in the harsh realities of daily struggle; hope that remains on intimate terms with death; hope that is life-renewing . . . .

—Cornel West, *Brother West: Living and Loving Out Loud*

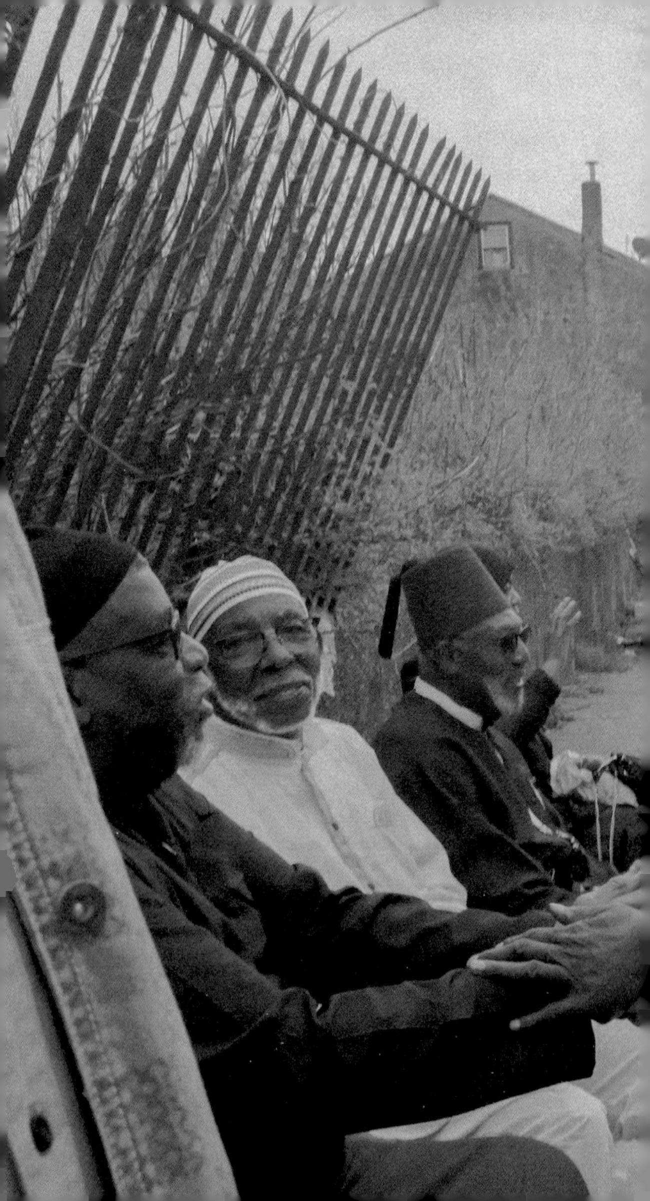

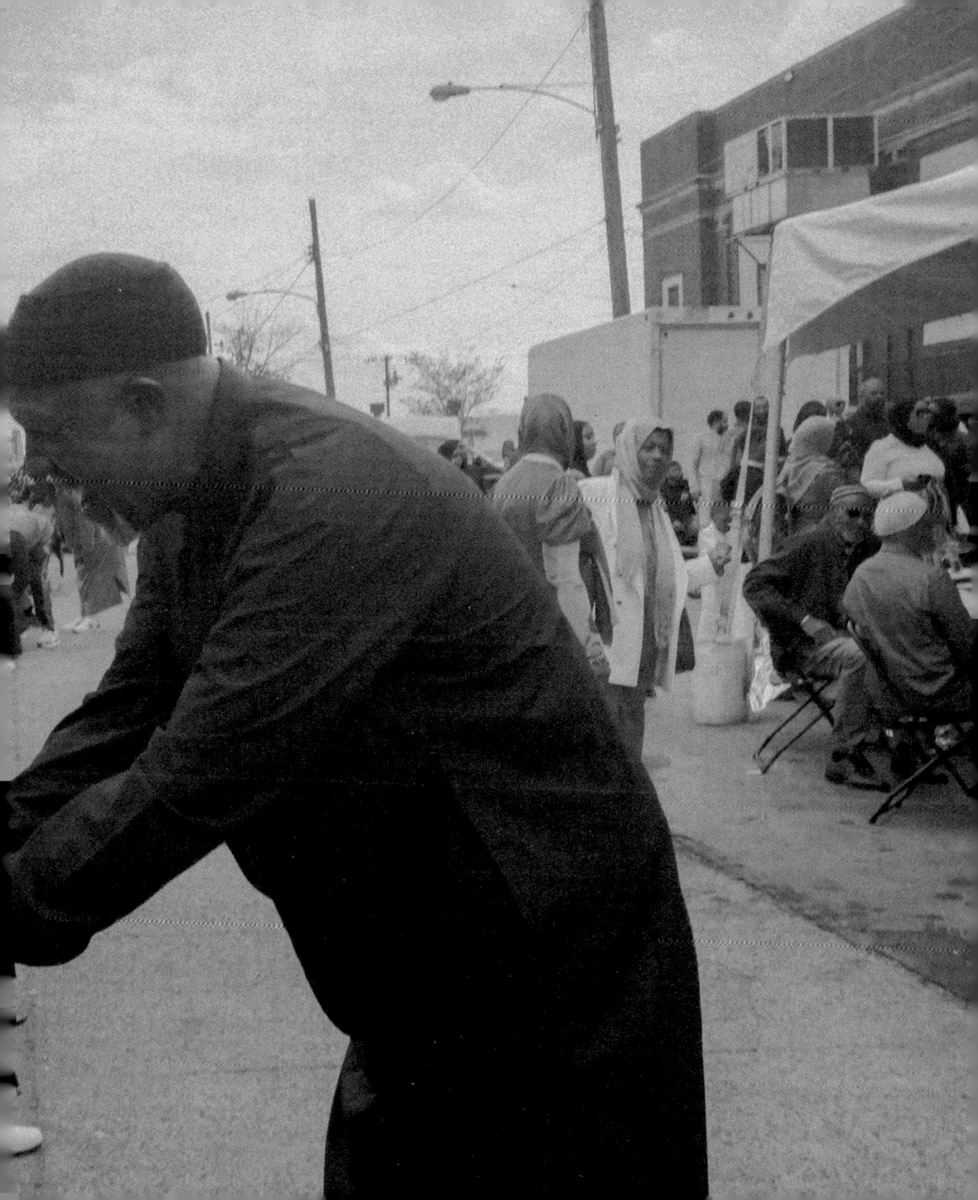

the ultimate faith in the justice of all things

I fell in love with that kind of music. I saw that to define music as something you listen to, something that pleases you, is very different from defining it as an instrument with which you can drive a point. In both instances, you can have the same song. But using it as an instrument makes it a different kind of music . . . somehow this music—music I could use as an instrument to do things with, music that was mine to shape and change so that it made the statement I needed to make—released a kind of power and required a level of concentrated energy I did not know I had. I liked the feeling.

—Bernice Johnson Reagon, "In Our Hands:
Thoughts on Black Music"

Rock, I don't go to church or the mosque like that (karim do) but that don't mean I ain't never felt God's presence. They too got something powerful over there in them spots. It's still something going on almost every other block 'round here. I agree with Kendrick Lamar most days but especially the day he said, "*Anytime I couldn't find God, I still could find myself through a song*." I think that's how it went.

I know them soul-stirring sorrow songs got some working answers for Us because there's this one record I've been entirely obsessed with. Like looped up for fifty-'leven long nights obsessed. And it's not just because of what's present in the recording, but also me stretching my listening to note what's not all there because it simply could never be. It's to honor the interesting Black magic of it all; we haven't and may just never figure it out. I probably need to take that truth to heart some more but I just rather keep listening, and listening, trying hard to insurgently imagine what all that something-inside-so-strong is.

Whatever was all happening up, down, and around this record may not have convinced me that you know Big J God exists, but more honest that there's still something liberating about the pursuit of the assumption that they do. At least it gotta be necessary for the folk present in that room. They embody real conviction, the kind my homie Ashon be telling me about, if only evident in the ephemeral mean—between time.

The song I'm talking about: Cory Henry and Kierra Sheard, "How Great Thou Art."

Yeah, yeah, my wife says I just never let the song finish. I feel like that's the point: I'm drawn to attempting to stay in it with them the whole time until it almost always overcomes me and I feel that I have to begin it all over again.

There's no moment in the music that you as a participating listener are left off the hook for seven minutes and thirty-three seconds. Everybody involved is rooted within performing and listening or better yet listening and performing the strongest of all what is inside for 7:33. A whole eight minutes, because you know how they do church records, they fade them out. Who knows how much longer the *feeling* really lasts.

Rock, there's a lot of things that I can't do for eight whole minutes. Not trying my hardest the whole time. You gotta maintain focus and care.

You gotta commit to discipline. You gotta be invested in precision. Sun Ra's favorite things he jazzed about in "Outer Spaceways Incorporated."

To achieve that angel race stuff? I swear that best be the benefits package of certifying your belief in the right kinda higher power—not just solely acknowledging their ethereal existence but getting so close with that soul-force that you might just share the controller for a lil' bit.

For eight whole minutes, I *feel* the constant and consistent shared belief embodied by their actions that this song we making together right here is gonna save souls. And Us deeply knowing that what we urgently desire most is a reminder that our songs can save souls. Like, really holding that this moment right here may be the only ever chance for Black liberation we ever gon' have so you better stay in there with it, with *Us*, and then make the most of it.

But Rock, let me land: the whole thing had to have begun with a deep practice of listening. Yeah, Kierra Sheard may have been the lead vocalist, but she exercised an enduring commitment of listening to them and possibly something beyond just all of them too that was physically present in that room. And Cory Henry—what can you say about him. GOAT.

I most clearly know that everyone in there chose to claim and keep themselves in on it until it really wasn't a *them* individually no more. Trust. It was a collective, revolutionary *we*. They all went with it and stayed in it together, which is the heaviest part—sustaining the presence of something freeing so close you can grasp at it. Being fully tapped in for and with each other's freedom, dreaming for another liberating kind of existence out there that just may never fully arrive or be fully proved. For eight whole minutes.

That might just be the closest we ever gonna get to the true and living Almighty.

Rock, what would it feel like to be all Black and bluesy and free like them for eight whole minutes? It gotta be worth being willing to pay tithes, amen-ing a couple thousand prayers, and establishing a congregation of folk to struggle with for a while.

At the end of the day, I know, in whatever ways we can invent, we got to find one sturdy handhold on this thing to each one pull one up outta this jawn. Might not even take eight whole minutes once we fully commit.

I think that what's contained in the blues is the African-American's cultural response to the world. We are not a people with a long history of writing things out; it's been an oral tradition: passing information, knowledge, ideas, and attitudes along orally. In order for the information to survive, you have to tell it in such a way that its memorable—so that someone else hearing the story will want to go and tell someone else. That's a way of ensuring its survival. One way to make that information memorable is to put it in a song. Music provides an emotional reference to the content of the song. The thing with the blues is that there's an entire philosophical system at work. And I've found whatever you want to know about the Black experience in America is contained in the blues. They couldn't stop 'em singing and passing along all their information in songs. This is what I've found the blues to be. So it is the Book. It is our sacred book. Every other people has a sacred book, so I claim it as that. Anything I want to know, I go there and find out.

—August Wilson, "Conversations with August Wilson"

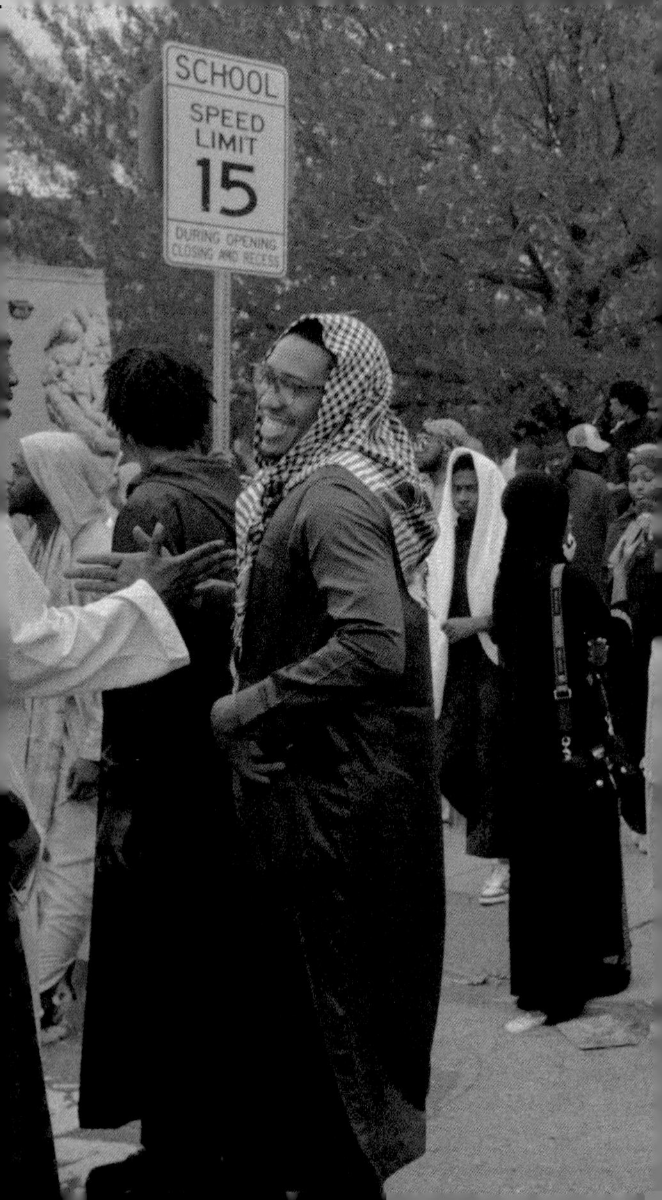
SCHOOL
SPEED LIMIT 15
DURING OPENING CLOSING AND RECESS

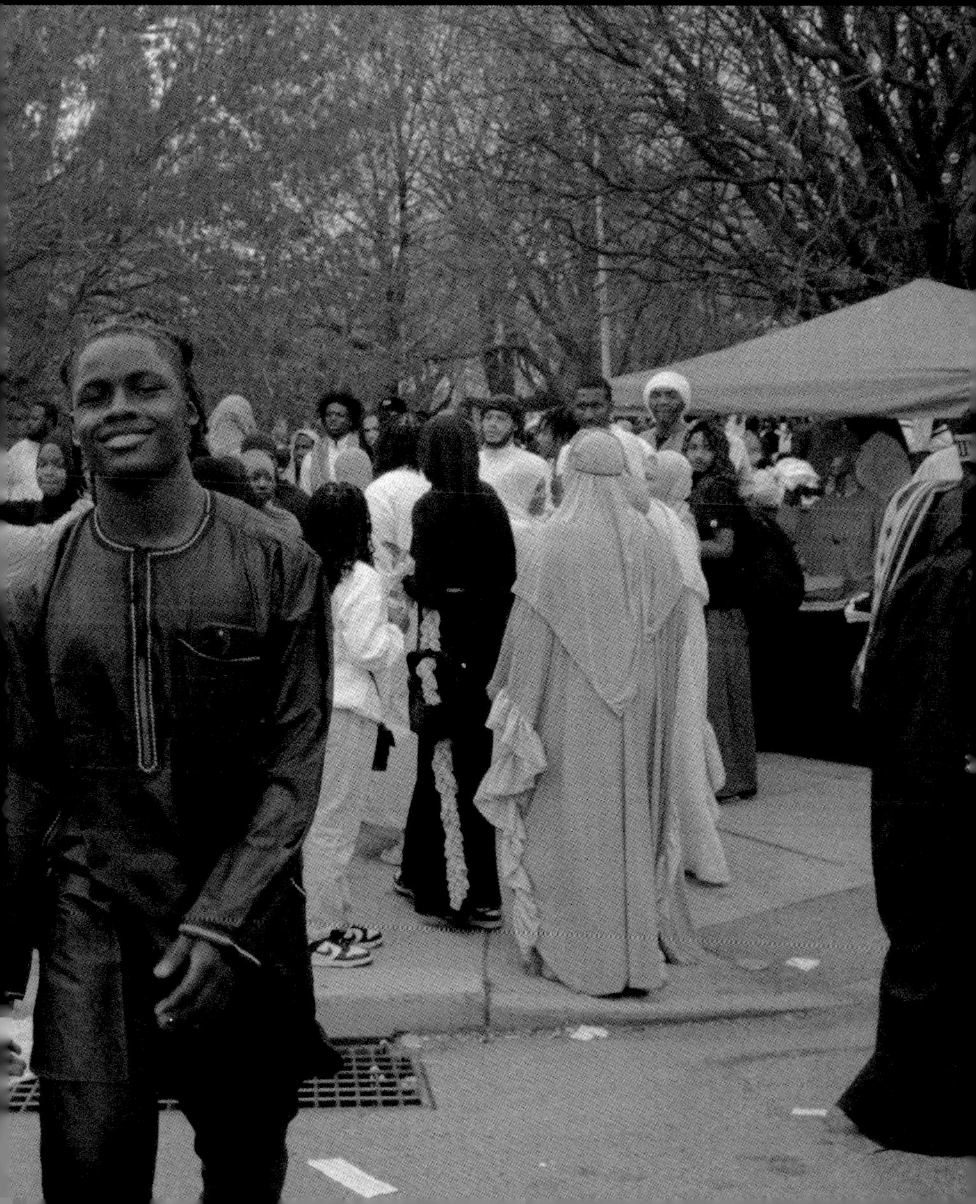

the slum village knows what love is

If there is anything I could offer young artists, I would say, be boldly where you want to be and really, really be *there.*

—Theaster Gates, "Sacralized Space: Theaster Gates on the Practice of Placemaking"

The ward, the Bottom, the ghetto—is an urban commons where the poor assemble, improvise the forms of life, experiment with freedom, and refuse the menial existence scripted for them.

—Saidiya Hartman, "The Terrible Beauty of the Slum"

How can we survive genocide? We can only address this question by studying how we have survived genocide. In the interest of imagining what exists there is an image of Michael Brown we must refuse in favor of another image we don't have. One is a lie, the other unavailable. If we refuse to show the image of a lonely body, of the outline of the space that body simultaneously took and left, we do so in order to imagine jurisgenerative black social life walking down the middle of the street—for a minute, but only for a minute, unpoliced, another city gathers, dancing. We know it's there, and here, and real; we know what we can't have happens all the time.

—Stefano Harney and Fred Moten, *All Incomplete*

Rock, our true smiles and our answers for the city are only made possible in, by, through impossibly sustained community. Impossible as a reminder that we exist without guarantees.

"It takes a village to raise a child" is not just a Malcolm X Park proverb. It's how we must stay free and survive. When we gather all Black and loud, when we celebrate the harvest of being each other's magnitude, business, and bond, I say as Miss Brooks said that we are wholly undetainable. We be a rough-ranked riot *beyond containment* like Claudia Jones. The genesis of our freedom recovered within a yearly carnival whether in Notting Hill or Port of Spain or Port Terminal, an under-planned church revival 'round Vernon Park near Germantown and Chelten, or a beloved Black Muslim Eid celebration off Lancaster Avenue at Clara Muhammad Park. You know, the one from that year we all remember because . . . yeah. *Asé.*

Rock, it takes a village, but what makes "the village"?

Black movement 'round here has always been subject to constant surveillance and ever-present strategies of repeated enclosure. This gets me flying down to the Caribbean, to the tradition of Carnival, where folk like M. NourbeSe Philip and Earl Lovelace challenge us to hear the triumphant culture of resistance to imperialism, colonialism, and racism embedded within its extravagant celebration of the oppressed city's fugitive pursuit to achieve unrestricted movement and our lasting Freedom Day. We will have our Freedom Day.

Rock, the late Julius S. Scott wrote in *The Common Wind*, "As long as masterless men and women found ways to move about and evade the authorities, they [the planter class] reasoned, these people embodied submerged traditions of popular resistance which could burst into the open at any time."

Yeah Rock, they know we coming. Uncle Paul says they know we be the decisive force. That's what they afraid of the most.

But like I been saying, I grew up in the City of Chester, four-and-a-half miles wide and a million undeserved tragic stories deep in it. It came to be one of the first European settlements on this side of the Black Atlantic, agreed to under an inevitably poisonous treaty made with the local Lenape Nation by the revered Quaker slave-owner

William Penn. The British reward to his father because he captured another colony for their Empire. We only have a place named Chester, Pennsylvania because a couple years before, the British colonizers captured Jamaica from the Spanish colonizers.

Most would say it bloomed, while most forget to say, "for white folks," in the early twentieth century when wartime industry exploded upon the Delaware River waterfront. When post-WWII deindustrialization hit the scene, it was abandoned by its big business corridor who blamed taxes and saw the opportunity to perfect their exploitation elsewhere. Most of its middle-class constituents, fearing association with the assembled poor, also searched for an elsewhere. We could be honest now and say it was some of Us too. Some of these folks think they really made it *out*, but all I see are visible scars.

Chester would become, post-WWII and all the wars after that, the place-trap in which Delaware County politicos decided it would entrap and enclose an emigrating Southern Black population searching for their own kind of illusory American dream.

In my lifetime alone, we struggled through the War on Drugs, a continuation of their long war on Us, the persistent imposition of waste companies [always with the state's permission] who tell us there is nothing wrong in the Chester air while they make billions burning Philadelphia and New York City's garbage and pay us in pennies and pollution. Our beloved Zulene Mayfield been sounding the alarm.

Rock, I live in Philly now, but have you ever been to New York City on a trash day? You know these trash-ass people just playing in our faces, just because they got some of our elected's friends on payroll. Meanwhile, our hospital was bought by private equity and ain't been right since. It was already being burned when it caught on fire a couple weeks ago. And now it's really gone.

I don't think the recession ever left my city, yet we continue to be left by that same crooked Pennsylvania state legislature already all ways permitting things that harm Us. Their newest game is sending in a Black overseer—I mean receiver whose sole role is to make sure the state receives their money. It's obvious why nobody likes his ass. He signed up for the job, I guess to keep his own Black family from ever living like we do. He chose to do the state's job.

Rock, folk got the nerve to ask me why I don't come home to run for office, like it's any real power in managing this third-class city in Pennsylvania that gets treated like every third-world country in the United Nations. Chester is the root of the third world within Us.

Seems like all we can do is keep sending in an elected state representative to beg big, toxic businesses, and toxic small ones too, to invest in our city as our sole—yes fiscal, but also possibly material—means of survival. I mean, that's if you consider City Hall the heart of the city.

> *Financial imperatives constantly try to reduce us all, despite ourselves, to the equivalent of pillagers, eyeing the world simply for what can be turned into money—and then tell us that it's only those who are willing to see the world as pillagers who deserve access to the resources required to pursue anything in life* other *than money. It introduces moral perversions on almost every level.*
>
> —David Graeber, *Debt: The First 5,000 Years*

Yet and still, there has and will continue to be a thin and yet kinda sturdy jurisgenerative Black aliveness that refuses to believe in my city's fiscal conclusions as the be-all, end-all purpose of our lives. Maybe that's why our finance people don't got accounting degrees. They was born yearning for a different kind of math more honest and nurturing to our lives.

Yet and still, the Black working-class culture of my city, the city I still to this day claim even as they all will read this and remind me I don't have a current mailing address there, we've remained abundantly gifted, talented, Black, and proud.

We produced tons of musical stars who never get all the money and accolades they deserve, scores of basketball legends who they cheated out the game (MJ ain't never had to play Zain Shaw), and most importantly, rebelliously thick, loving Black family assemblages (because we all related somehow) committed to striving, rehearsing, and performing decent, dignified lives. This how we roll to even the odds against the master's narrative of systematic injustice and premature death.

It is in this way, in the humble and sincere, constant but not always visible city activities of our schoolteachers, our ball coaches, our preachers and pastors, our nurses (so many nurses), our artists and they side hustles, our activists and their impossible demands, our caregivers and their other-mothering, plus a host of a whole lot of other real important folk who don't be getting their credit in these lists, that we have been able to discover or distill or rediscover fifty-eleven ways to remain vividly and dangerously Black and alive.

We flex even further by crafting shared spaces of insurgent joy, manufactured from everyday double dares of improvised reinvention, like selling snow and/or snowballs, dodging the unlivable destinies that is at all times inevitably placed in front of Us and charging it to the game.

Rock, they stay forgetting the ways we have continuously strived for excellence, in spite of all what those folk who stay indifferent to our lives and always actively creating new traps, obstacles, and loopholes be saying about and doing to us.

It's like them folk can't hear those sounds, our sounds, our true Black blues. Ellison might say they just remain oblivious to recognize that our Black livelihoods reside on those lower, otherwise frequencies. But we stay attuned. We stay in tune. We keep on the one. We remember Us.

"Be safe. Text me when you get home." A common gathering exit refrain that us Chester folk say. In a city rife with multiple scales of violence and viral legacies of communal trauma, you never know what might be around the corner. We live with that "around the corner" fear on the daily basis. It is infused into Chester High's dim hallways, the greased food platters at Showell's, and certainly it's all up in the residue of the bar table at Hayes Lounge. We know the only way to assuage that fear is through impossibly sustained gestures of rebellious care.

I hear the storm. They talk to me about progress, about 'achievements'; diseases cured, improved standards of living. I am talking about societies drained of their essence, cultures trampled underfoot, institutions undermined, lands confiscated, religions smashed, magnificent artistic creations destroyed, extraordinary possibilities wiped out.

They throw facts at my head, statistics, mileages of roads, canals, and railroad tracks.

I *am talking about thousands of men sacrificed to the Congo-Ocean.* I am talking about those who, as I write this, are digging the harbor of Abidjan by hand. I am talking about millions of men torn from their gods, their land, their habits, their life—from life, from the dance, from wisdom. I am talking about millions of men in whom fear has been cunningly instilled, who have been taught to have an inferiority complex, to tremble, kneel, despair, and behave like flunkeys. They dazzle me with the tonnage of cotton or cocoa that has been exported, the acreage that has been planted with olive trees or grapevines. I am talking about natural economies that have been disrupted-harmonious and viable economies adapted to the indigenous population—about food crops destroyed, malnutrition permanently introduced, agricultural development oriented solely toward the benefit of the metropolitan countries, about the looting of products, the looting of raw materials.*

They pride themselves on abuses eliminated.

I too talk about abuses, but what I say is that on the old ones—very real—they have superimposed others—very detestable. They talk to me about local tyrants brought to reason; but I note that in general the old tyrants get on very well with the new ones, and that there has been established between them, to the detriment of the people, a circuit of mutual services and complicity. They talk to me about civilization, I talk about proletarianization and mystification. . . .

I make a systematic defense of the societies destroyed by imperialism.

—Aimé Césaire, "Between Colonizer and Colonized"

Care can be found in the way that we wish everyone a safe trip home, yet more expansively, it can be found in the way we look to one another for a reminder of our own absolution when there's so much beyond our control. We step in to one another's struggles. Make sure that everyone has a plate to eat at the Chester Park cookout. Make sure that everyone has something to sip on at Chester High Homecoming.

When one of us loses someone close in our family, there are group texts and real-life group chats wishing them well and asking them if anything is needed. When funeral costs are overwhelming, as they so assuredly are, local funeral directors pledge reasonably doubtful to be reconciled payment schedules and other extended families reach out to many of the city's beloved independent businesses to host a donation jar.

In my city, during our whole city's graduation week, well-wishers stand from the front porch and nod, smile, congratulate, give it up to the new cohort of Chester's future hanging out the window of they momma's car with they ratchet-ass friends.

Ain't none of us forgot we live in dark, suspect, untrustful times. Yet we refuse to succumb to believing that everyone around us all the time is a threat to our imposed and foretold demise.

Well, in a way that might not be true for all of Us all of the time. You can't call it sometimes. Sometimes life gets the best of Us and we lose hold of the wheel but not the trigger on a stolen .38. I'm lying, it's usually a .22.

Rock, remind me. We gotta get some but not all these guns off the street. And I don't mean just the young ones either. We be outside dying inside.

In this chaotic, confusing, definitely stupid yet unpredictably harmful 2025 political moment we find ourselves in, there is much that the world could gain from standing witness to how we Chester folk be doing more than just surviving with the little bit of earth and big hearts of gritty love we be having. That we be having more than we can ever present the provenance suggesting what we own.

Even though what they do is wrong, just maybe we imagined our grace. Maybe we stole it. A distinction without a difference.

> *'Run your race,' they told Us at my ninth grade orientation assembly. 'Because guess what, this school has a 32 percent drop-out rate. You know what that means? Look to your left . . . look to your right . . . one of y'all is not going to make it.'*

The school was Chester High School, at the time the only place in the city (still the only one worthy of one's respect) where you could attend public high school in the Chester Upland School District. This made it both a cherished tradition of ours and burden with an infamous reputation. One could not be a true "Chesterite" (*Rock, no one from Chester says that*) without being located within the collective memories of the school.

"What class you from?" These are questions still on the top of everyone's mind when we run into each other. Our Chester High Homecoming celebration is unlike any other, much like our generalized condition as well. Each graduating class sets out a tent at the still-needs-renovation athletic field with abundant libations and flagrant music. We be at the A-Field to see who amongst Us will flex the hardest.

Last year, it was '99. 2025, it was us. '06. '99 do be winning because they be putting in for public/private caterers so that the many mothers, fathers, full-time workers, caregivers, and the don't-be-working-at-all could put up their feet, swig a bit of Henny, and dance to the classic flagrant twerk music of their time. *Cash Money Records owns more than just '99 and 2000.*

Chester High School was the place, territorially, where neighborhood kids with long histories of tensions would meet. These could emerge from all matter of things: a hard foul, a roasting session that verily went too far, a stolen bike that went missing from its original thief, a teenage Black girl who gave her phone number to two different niggas from two different hoods, etc.

All this everyday struggle led to many, many neighborhood squabbles, many instances of fisticuffs from Saturday's night house parties resurfacing in a Tuesday fourth-period lunch block. These were ultimately the scheduled but unpredictable fights that caused the scene I offered before from the newly leaving principal. The beginning of their end, ritualized as why our school and our city would "never get right." Because y'all ghetto and got no self-control.

Bubbling up under the surface of those truths, there was an even bigger struggle at hand. Our schools were always under the dirty thumb of the state's control in my memory. The records say 1994. Yet the state never cared to make sure that our schoolteachers—like my mother—could count on their salary increases or worse, that students could count on being able to have a textbook to take home. It got so bad one year that the teachers asked our moms and some pops to buy paper to bring in as part of our school supplies list just so they could print out copies of the week's lessons. That's only if the copier didn't jam that week.

In the merry-go-round that was our rotating school district leadership, no one was allowed—or actually succeeded—in trying to deeply question the ever-diminishing returns in funding that would come from the state. They told Us it was our fault.

It was really the fault of the police. Well, not the police department itself, though yes, they inflated their pensions with sketchy overtime assignments. It was more our overall commitment to the nonsense of policing as having sense for Us. If we as a city are going to accept any part of the blame, let it be for that. Now, because of the police's drawin'-ass actions, we don't have any sense at all. And the overseer-receiver trying to sell the Water Company, again. Our overseer-receiver need his money to give to his boss so his kids might get a free education from the state.

Yeah, the overwhelming dysfunction that anchored our virtually all-Black schools, in all of its obvious precarity that I can visibly remember and yet not ever remain stuck on. Under the burden of all that, we were advised as ninth-grade students and Black baby-children to keep our blinders to ALL this and "run your race."

Subdued while in school, the little boy opened up like an umbrella outdoors, in the street, at home. Everything outside the school became an even bigger school. What counted was his busy inner life: things that interested him, things he cared about, things the Teachers never knew were there. He was bundled into reading and writing when he knew nothing about himself, or life, or grownups, or the world they were bringing to him.

—Patrick Chamoiseau, *School Days*

"Run," they told us, Rock. They made it their job to oversee-receive it, which only lasted two years most the time, to keep Us running.

—

One of the most beautiful things about my city's Chester High Homecoming is witnessing two Chester folk that you knew had on-sight beef back in the day shake hands, toast drinks, and look yet come to find out they kids' playin' on the same pee-wee basketball team this season. There's an enduring respect that can come from standing witness to shared struggle and strategies of Black striving, when due diligence of high heat is allowed to run its course.

Rock, again, we got to figure out how to get some, but not all, these guns off the street.

The beauty of being all-up-in Chester High Homecoming Week is a reminder we give ourselves: none of us really chose to be here, in this city that was dumped on Us (too real), and became our city. It's not like picking a college or even something like a principled political pursuit. It's kinda happenstance we all ended up being raised in this city—my city, our city—and had to practice manufacturing Black magic to survive this enclosure. This state controlled public school district, set in our yes-it-would-be-fiscally-responsible-to-file-for-bankruptcy city experience, was tenuously held together by knots of hock spit, rolls of duct tape, lottery ticket pipedreams, and the courageous, undying Black love of a few praying grandmothers.

And at homecoming, no one from Chester really cares if you can present the official paperwork that certifies you as a Chester High School graduate. We was all there; we remember Us.

The gift of the city, my city, our city, is that we—in spite of it all—we too damn often do choose, sometimes even against our more best rational selves, to come together year after year to celebrate the fact that we did, do, and will survive this whole war made against Us of no historical fault of our own.

We do and will, but always in a way where it still will hurt a whole hell of a lot and that hurt might not ever simply fade away. It's gonna stay there and remain sore until the end (which again, is really our beginning). We won't fully know in advance, but there's a chance, a real chance, we can *feel* it and feel ourselves *out*. For real this time.

Facing all that, Rock, we give of ourselves and still strive to recover all those here physically, and spiritually and otherwise, the ones who make with us and the ones who made for us the oh-so-thin-but-not-so-frail chance at realizing our full Black freedom.

But it's something about losing yourself to that Chester sound, in a crowd of everybody you grew up with, discovering that right beat at that right time to "dance our way out of our constrictions," like the Funkadelic song says.

It was a mess, as usual. It was yet our Black life. It was Us knowing in our bodies but not always the mind where we had fully been. It was Us, stretching that moment to muster surviving beats of Black joy and plot the unplanned rebellion.

Because ain't none of Us know what was coming around the corner. But we knew that this time right now was and always is fragile, precious, golden, fleeting. And we knew we had to hold on to that. We had to flow with it. We knew that these moments was what made us, Us. And in us being Us, there's all we need if we can only stay focused on what freedom we supposed to want if we do indeed really, really want to be well.

Rock, maybe I'm on this here because homecoming was last week. It was life. It was a mess, but our city's kind of beautiful mess. I jumped off the Wilmington Line at Chester Transportation Center, dropped in on my cousin's barbershop before heading over to the A-Field. One quick Uber ride in a beat-up Dodge Caravan and I emerged out the back end of Showalter STEM High School and onto Concord Road.

My classmates, the illustrious, unfuckwittable Class of 2006, was supposed to be holding down a tented-up parking spot with the grill and a cooler. With our drinks already on ice. With our burgers already heating up.

I got there and there was no grill to be found. No tent. Not even a damn table. Just a cold, huddled-up group of our former all-star cheerleaders trying to stay warm and be warm.

This was supposed to be one of them good days. We was off, Rock.

I looked from whence my help shall come. Fortunately, my sister is Class of 2005, and they had brought their own, but kinda everybody's DJ booth to the homecoming tailgate. Chelsea poured me up a cup of woo juice somebody had made but not fully described within a retrofitted gallon-size Hawaiian Punch container.

Nah, Rock, no, I ain't ask what was in it. They call you a coward and laugh at you for that kind of behavior. You suppose to just bask in they generosity and be merry, dance with the DJ for a song or two, don't draw, and if you not Class of '05 for real, keep it moving.

My youngin', Rebel Foster, had just arrived to take over their—but obviously kinda ours too—turntables. We go back a ways. I remember when he first started DJing up Swarthmore for drunk, drugged, bugged-out white kids who often too voyeuristically loved our music. Them parties was something else. He figured out how to sustain that Chester sound through it all.

Rebel Foster hit the Class of 2005's mix board with some Chester classics: Ying Yang Twins, ol' 504 Boyz; Choppa Style. That New Orleans Bounce was always in my city, Rock. I remember the rent parties I found myself out to as a youngin' where them songs played as I would try my self-depressing-best to be deserving of and useful in a wallie with some jawn that I may have only known because their gym class got out before mine entered at Smedley Elementary.

We all stood witness at Chester High Homecoming to one another searching for true smiles, remembering the good ol' days when our striving, styling, and profiling was all that mattered. *I know no one talks like that no more.*

But it's true these days, we all a bit more bogged down. The presence of multiplying bills, mouths to feed, and insufficient workplaces that practice faulty math can really weigh Us down. Like, you can physically see it, and I don't mean our birthmarks nor body weight.

In spite of it all, Rock, it's still something about losing yourself to that Chester sound, in a crowd of everybody you grew up with, trying to find that right beat to "dance our way outta these constrictions," like the record says. It's gonna be a mess. We gonna get wet. But it's always going to be giving life.

Us *feeling* where we had been, not quite knowing but *feeling* all what carried us through, and simultaneously tensed with where we had yet to go. Practicing and rehearsing striving together, choosing and claiming our place, two-stepping to let it all loose with spontaneous simplicity.

Chester High Homecoming is Us, subtended by Black music's hidden moment of truths to unveil the secret flash in the spirit of our inexhaustible surviving Black joy.

Because none of us ever know what be coming around the corner. We must know that this time, and too much of our time is fragile yet precious, golden yet fleeting. It's hard to score out here, in the midst of the state's daily offense. We only get a couple shots; we gotta make our free throws.

Rock, championships against the state can be won by free throws. Remember Stonewall. Remember the riots.

So, Rock, we Chester people knew we had to clamp down on to Black music for dear life; for our dear Black lives. We Chester folk knew that these moments surrendering ourselves to this tooted-up booty music was what made us, Us. And this Village of Us was all we needed to practice, preserve, and promote to serve as the ultimate answer to our more beautiful, more terrible histories in this undeserving-ass sack of lies, which is this obviously and inevitably dying country. A dying colonial country that might not have a future in my city; let's be honest, it's never been something the city needed. It's never been for Us.

We take C-Pride in staying with the trouble, staying in the nitty-gritty of our too-thick versions of Black love, with the city—my city, our city, which is kinda everybody's city, if you really, really be there.

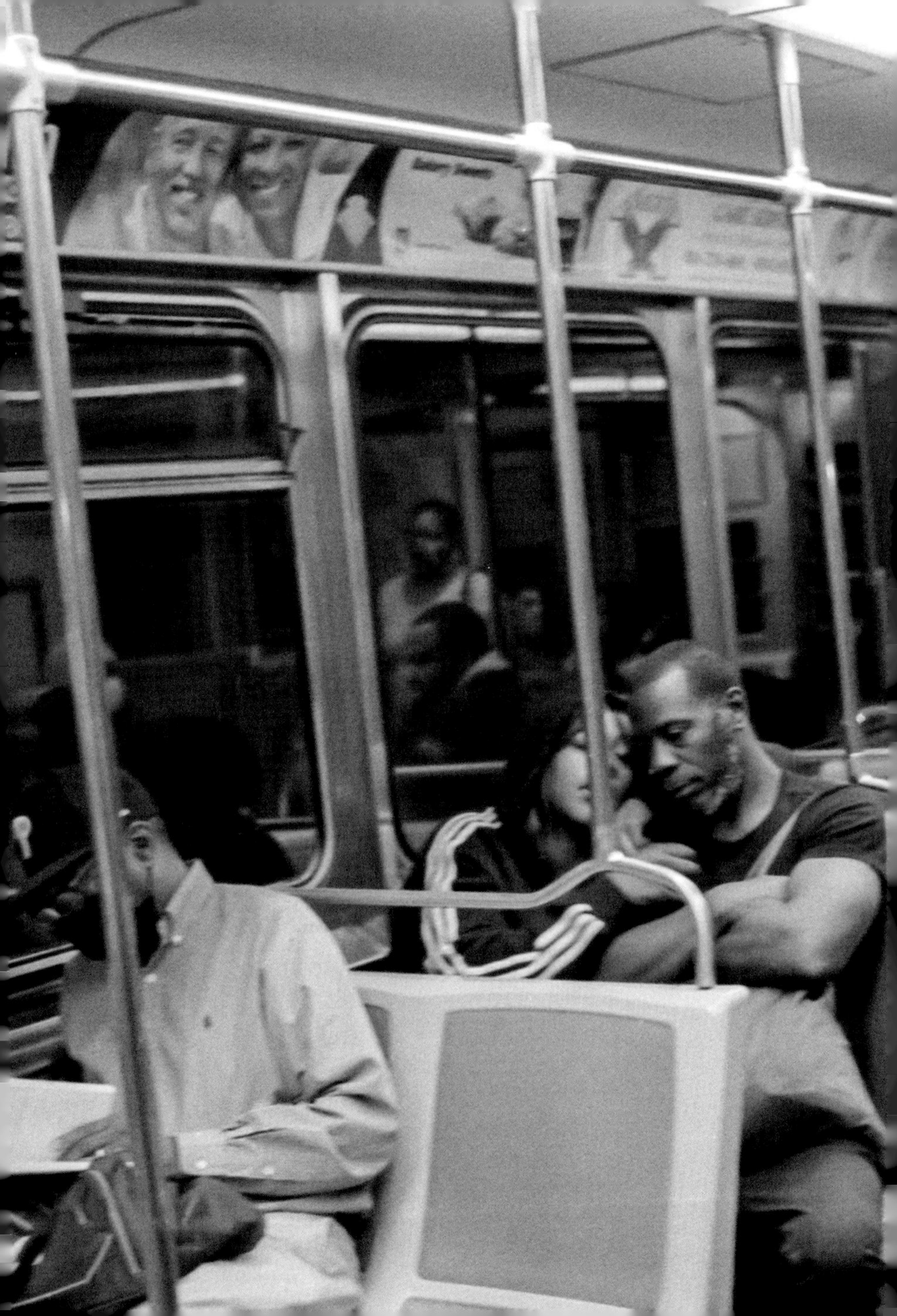

We love what we have, no matter how little, because if we don't, everything will be gone. If we don't, we will no longer exist, since there will be nothing here for us. What's here is something that we are still building. It's something we cannot yet see, because we are part of it.

Someday soon, this building will stand on its own, while we, we will be the trees that protect it from the fierce wind, the trees that will give shade to children sleeping inside or playing on swings.

—Mosab Abu Toha, "We Love What We Have"

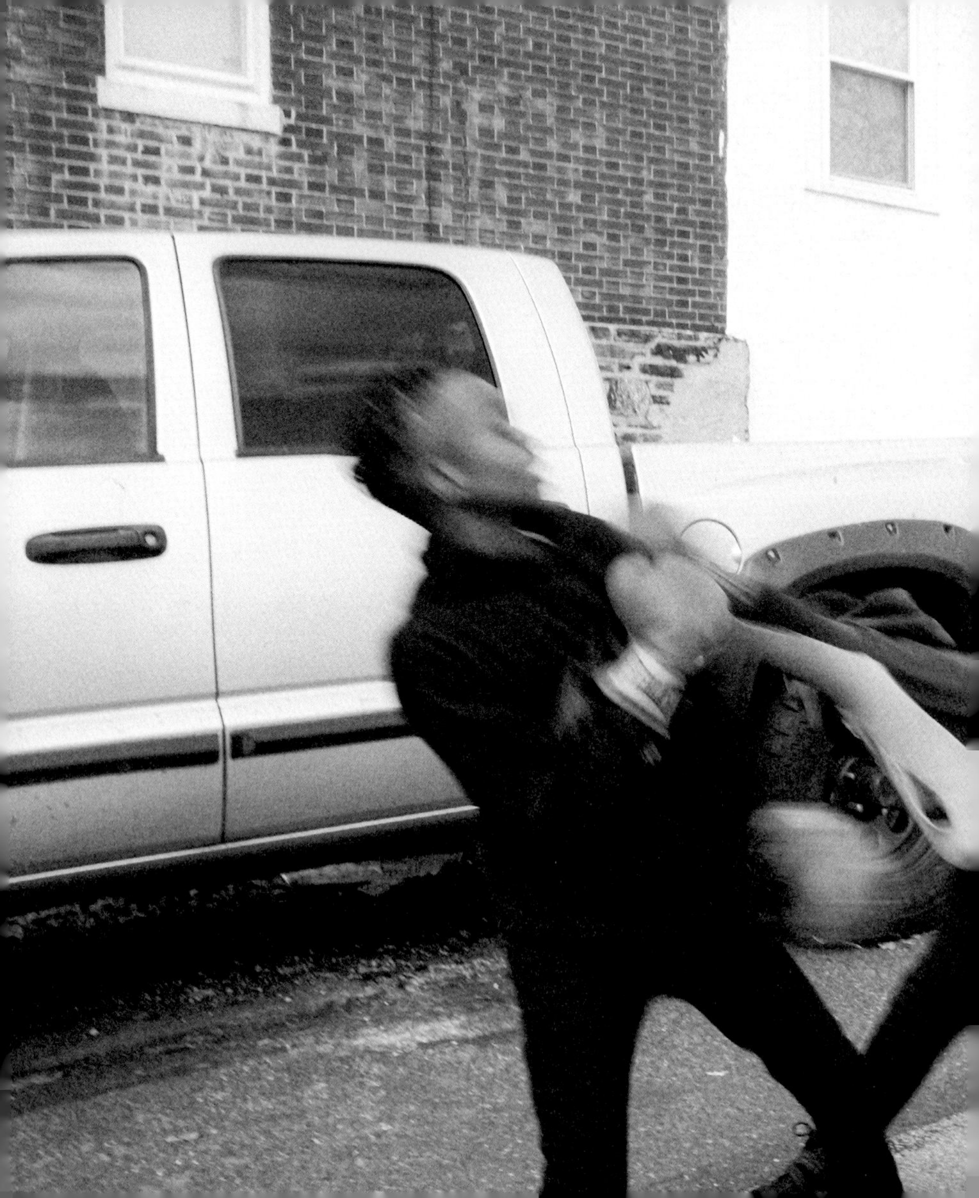

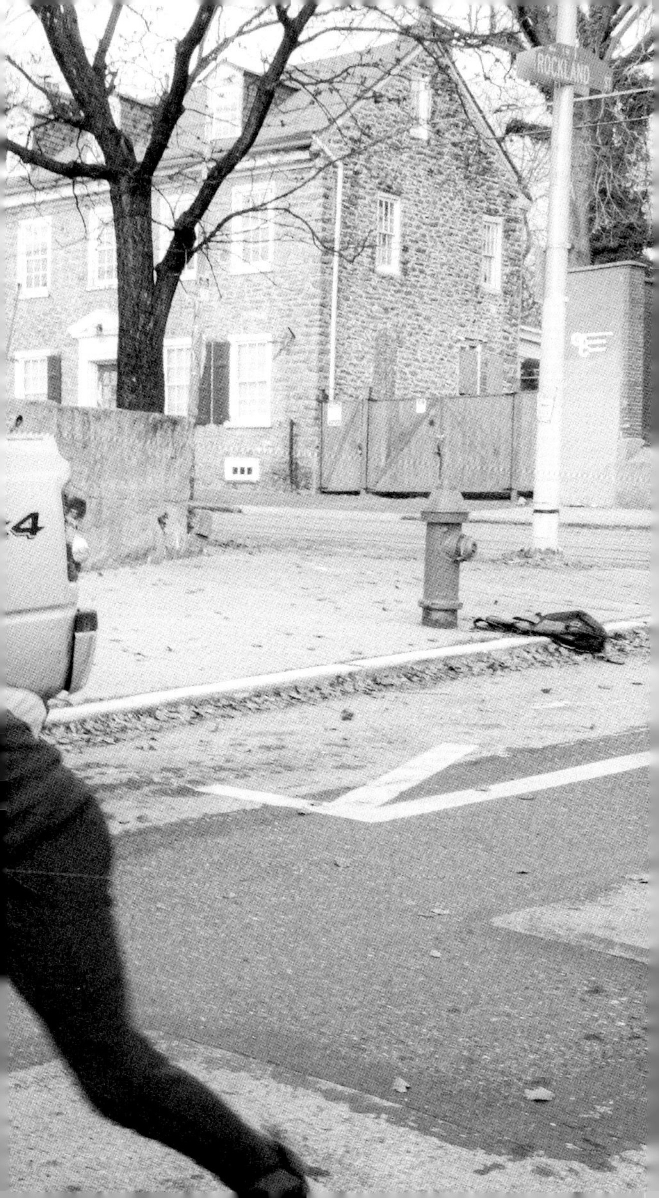
ROCKLAND

be a man

Lot of times, it ain't what you saying, it's what you not saying . . .

—Freeway, featuring Black Thought, "Keep Winning"

As we come to the tail end of this Rock, I keep reflecting back to this one thing this child who was in my class told me: "You don't let us be kids, Chris." Yeah, we was at a Quaker school, where they allow kids to call you by your first name. *Mama Gail always says kids are just baby goats and we need to change our language if only for the time we are in her company.*

But I thought to myself in that moment that I, in my kind of helpless advocacy, wanted for them young folks to be more aware of the impact of the choices they made and can make, if I stood to just play back the tape with them a little bit to witness. I didn't know that childhood was supposed to be this protected space of unknowing. I felt like I didn't have that growing up. Like Gil Scott, I didn't know I came from a broken home.

Take this. When I was in the seventh or eighth grade in Chester, my house was raided, the outcome of a years-long federal investigation of my cousins, because they were more successful than many others in our city at making a way when they said there was no way. And I'm not trying to dismiss nor glorify some of the violent, harmful choices they made trying to hold on to that way and those means. And yeah, I'd rather, because I know they would do the same for me: to accentuate the agency of their choices rather than the overdetermined structural conditions. There's another time for that necessary context. And a long book about the Highland Gardens has already been written.

But this sting operation we talking about is one of them just before dawn, with the M4 assault rifles, high-tech shields, and with lights-but-no-bodycams type of raids. They must have been hella prepared because the organizational chart was in the *Delco Times* the same morning it occurred. At least that's how soon I remember it, because no one in school that day believed that me, the smart quiet kid with thick glasses and thrift-store Polo, could be somehow entangled within these insurgent Chester Street dreams and nightmares. *I mean, I really wasn't. My family would never let me. My cousins made sure of it by dropping us off early and telling us when not to look.*

That dawn, they knocked just like the damn police, and I just so happened to be the first one from my three siblings that made it to the door. But I'm twelve or thirteen. The pigs go, "POLICE OPEN UP," and I'm only in my boyhood boxer draws, like "hold up, we need a minute."

They didn't give us a minute. They immediately took their battering ram to the front door of our home before I could find some pants, revealing themselves to me as the new, true, heavily armed Bad Boys. No Martin Lawrence. That woke everybody else up. My siblings: fourteen, fifteen, and seven, and my pops, who also didn't have time to find his pants so he now too in the living room in his tighty-whities.

Looking back, he might've intentionally chose to show his ass.

Now, these must have been the from-out-of-town pigs, because they are rummaging through our whole house, just in every room, flipping shit that wouldn't even make sense as the solution in this often still-too-fatal, hide-and-seek game they playing. If they knew anything about my family for real—well, at least the one side—they would know we ain't the type of Chester niggas who gon' be hiding under no bed.

They wasn't there. Some nights before that I sincerely wished they was home more. But their type of work is a road game. Most of them home now tho.

So they have finally stopped breaking up enough of all our hard-earned home furniture, and now all of a sudden, they want to use their words. Talking with my dad, still in his tighty-whities, about the whereabouts of his nephews. Nobody knows. And my dad had his own parenting issues, of course, but he raised us right enough to know we ain't gonna be no damn snitches to nobody other than them.

They finally give up on his obfuscation and leave out the broken-down opening where the front door of our family's home used to be before they arrived. *Funny enough, Rock, we sold the house years ago but the door we replaced it with is still the door at the address when I drive through.*

In the wake of their chaos, exiting back onto the streets of Chester, my dad sat up right there in his dingy tighty-whities to say just this first thing to his adolescent son:

> "But why you ain't just open the damn door when they first said something?"

And then he proceeded to remind all his kids that we was still going to school that day.

Rock, no lie, we all still went to school that day. It could be he was afraid too of not going to work. Maybe he too didn't know what to do with what we just experienced. An escape hatch was to fall back on his familiar rhythm, head to his desk job that morning in Wilmington, and then back to Ginn's at 2nd and Kerlin Streets that evening for another nightcap with the kitchen lady.

I ain't forgot that morning, so I know there's still something there to sit with, to make sense of, to derive from and distill some usable truths. I reflect on this and my Chester childhood, and I refuse the imposition that it is all clouded with only Black childhood trauma. A good-enough fiction I can live with is that this moment informed my grasp on a steely Arkansas-borne Black blues resilience, only activated by growing up working-class and Black in this kind of American chaos. And taking a stand, no matter how naive. Show your ass. Funk it up.

The words "y'all still going to school today . . ." form a minor dissonant note necessary for moving us forward, an up-South Black father's desperate, fragile, sorrow-stained yet necessary warning that the unpredictable traumatic violence of the pig system is, in all ways, trying to make a spectacle for your full attention when it's better contained in your rearview, behind the priorities of Us planning for what's ahead. A father's plea to not let it swallow you whole and lose your own sense of becoming. Don't end up at Ginn's trying to run and hide, drinking fantasies in the illusion of flight.

They can fuck up your furniture, but don't let them steal your soul. Go to school. Be with your people. Focus on your studies. Don't get caught up in the four walls. Focus on building up. Focus on building Us up.

Never known if my pops had access to articulate those lessons he shared with Us, him being his eldest sister's baby brother and navigating the loss of his own parents, I reckon before the family ever migrated up-South from West Helena, Arkansas. He too caught up in the fragments of memories, the precarity and risky foreclosure of Black freedom dreams in a hostile world. It's easier to write this fiction with him no longer physically here. Still, objects in the rearview mirror always remain closer than they appear.

I gotta tell you this, Rock, we had our issues at times, but my pops did his big one by showing up to grab his children after his separated-but-not-divorced wife transitioned way too early for our liking. He showed up. He might've not had the tools—he had to have known this on the road there. But he showed up. He got wet. That provides Us a working answer for sure.

I might not have survived if he didn't take that eight-hour drive down I-95 to North Carolina. Got me a Ruff Ryders CD too, on the way home, at a time I should not have been listening to any volume of Ruff Ryders. We went with my cousin Cindy to Powerhouse that year and saw Beanie Sigel's perform his live response to the Lox.

Rock, for the young Black man examining himself in the mirror, get real comfortable with the prayer of serenity, composing your own future without apology nor complaint, and don't go telling everybody our business. Our life is a war and it's your role to keep up the good fight. Show your ass. But show up for Us. Learn it to the youngbouls.

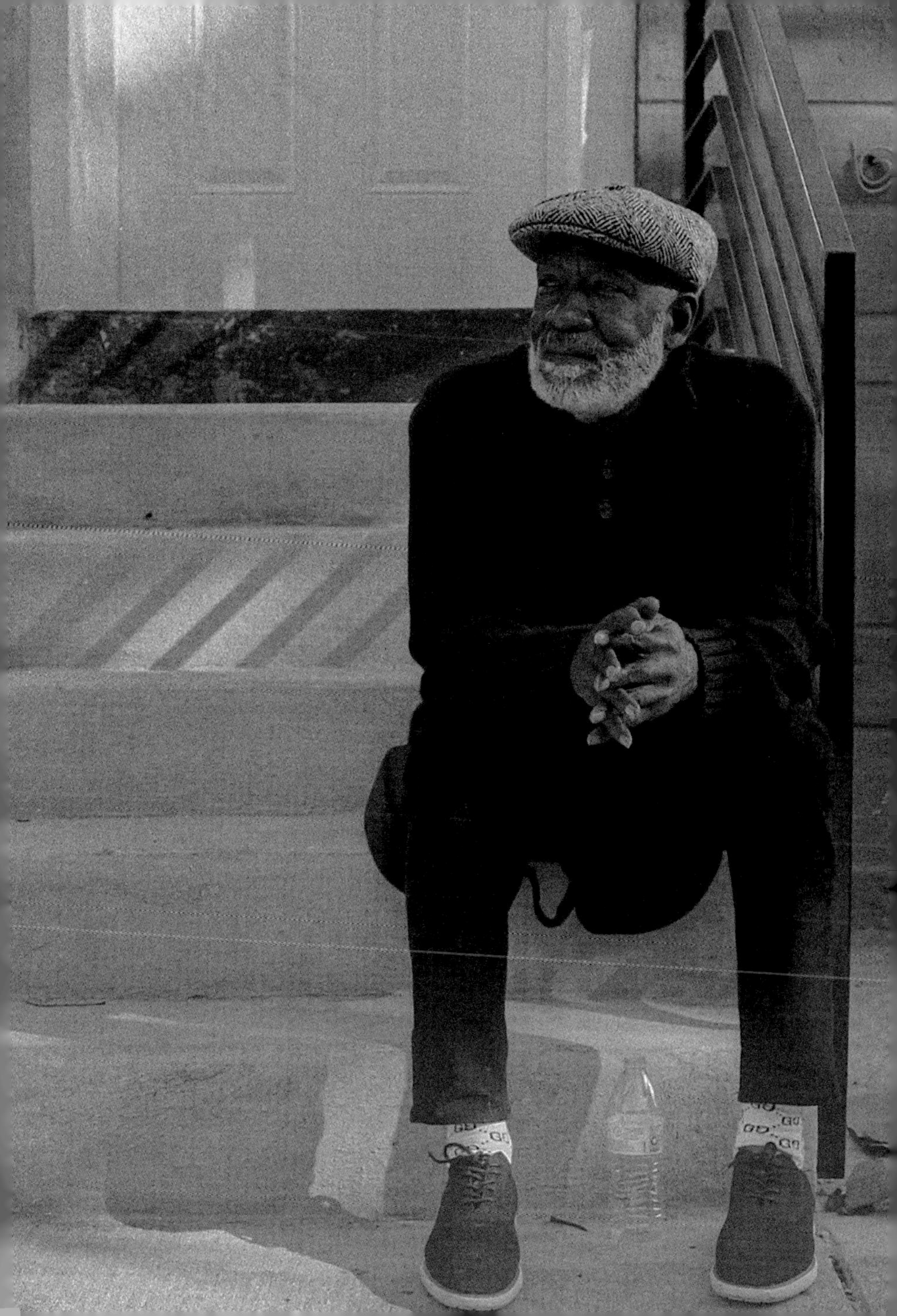

inner(re)visions

In my own sloppy work, on and off the page, I was beginning to understand 'revision' as a dynamic practice of revisitation, premised on ethically reimagining the ingredients, scope, and primary audience of one's initial vision. Revision required witnessing and testifying. Witnessing and testifying required rigorous attempts at remembering and imagining. If revision was not God, revision was everything every God ever asked of believers.

—Kiese Laymon, "What we owe and are owed"

Rock, my moms and pops transitioned to ancestors pretty early in my life. Mom right after my thirteenth birthday. My dad, 'round sixteen, or how I time it, eleventh grade at the High.

Yes, my mother, a schoolteacher in the Chester Upland School District, succumbed to a resurgent form of breast cancer while I was heading into the seventh grade, and years later, my bar-friendly—possibly still suffering before that—father came down with severe liver complications and met eternal rest after a more than month-long hospital stay while I was in the eleventh grade. This my truth, not just my idea of ancestry.

There was myself, my older brother, older sister, and my younger sister left to figure out what to do in the wake. How to defend our dead that remained alive within Us.

There was, and is, still much gratitude to be given the massive Chester presence of cousins, aunts, uncles, family friends, classmates, and all the other folk who don't be getting they credit on these lists, who played a central role in the village that covered and created the path for us to find our own way to some sense of self-sufficiency, if there is such a thing for any of Us individually.

And maybe, for being the beneficiary of all that sometimes, too-thick Black love, I'm willing to go down within the hold of the clipper ship, even if it kills me. I'm a ride or die with my city.

Yet, Rock, even then in the wake of that amateur accounting of self-sufficiency, it remains an open boat space that every Black boy baby-child must recognize, confront, claim, and ultimately decide for themselves who they will sail on to become. You still got to make that choice.

Just maybe, in the absence of my parents' direct and physically present words, I experimented on deep listening strategies while home on my DSL-enabled Dell computer for how to imagine, invent, and author plots of what I believe they might just be saying, you know, essentially. Because essentially, to claim this is also to put forward a half-truth of who I know they really, really were.

Like, if I'm being honest, I ain't forgot that my pops had really made us split the bill for the internet upgrade. I was fourteen. But he knew we wasn't going back to no dial-up; I had too many downloads running in the queue. I made it work, selling bootleg CDs in the hallways of the High. And ring tones. Remember them? I would really be up all night, soul searching for, with, and in music.

Rock, my idea of mom and pops as *they who gave me life*, my then-and-now ancestor parents, becomes in this improvised, unrehearsed process irreducible to who I solely could *rememory* them to be.

Portland's own Mitchell S. Jackson put the process of composing composite parents like this:

> And if a boy is not blessed with a father or gifted with a dynamic stand-in then he must find ways to make one. He must identify the father*ish* men in his life, find what he needs from them, and compose one. . . . It is an act of necessity and I should know. . . .
>
> Pops was a group of men who provided a loving example of what it would soon enough mean to be a man. Pops nurtured me. Bestowed me with his wisdom. Pushed me to nuance the way I saw the world. He inspired me to dream. He tended my harms. He made sure I knew it was in me to surpass him.

What I uncovered through the words and life of Mitchell S. Jackson is an immediate mirror and slow lens of what it may have meant for me to search for these ancestral examples in order to fulfill a human need: claiming purpose in the everyday struggle to survive.

Remember, Rock, I told you how important Toni Morrison is. She said the only grace we could have was the grace we could *imagine*. I obviously feel her, but we might just need to *feel* it in the air too.

I feel like somewhere in there, Rock, somewhere in dealing with all that, I grasped the essence of the concealed weapon that is being-with Black music. A record like Jay-Z's *Blueprint*; Scarface's *The Fix*; Lupe Fiasco's *Food & Liquor*; Lauryn Hill's still-underrated *MTV Unplugged 2.0*; "Everything" by Little Brother. This music might have saved my life. A notable quotable gave the gesture of possible proverb, hint, clue under the backbeat, if you could bend your ear past all the ignorant shit. Yeah, weighing it all on my consciousness, and nobody believes me when I say I hate the prison of conscious rap.

The thing about loss is that you don't lose someone once. You lose someone a first initial time. That is the inciting event. And if you live long enough without them, you go on to lose them repeatedly, for as long as you're alive and they're not. And that means that you have to get accustomed to burying someone repeatedly. Which, if not thought of in a way that is generous, can be too daunting to live with. But on the other hand, if you believe as I do, that grief is an emotion that's knocking on the door of memory, and asking you to recall something, then there's real gratitude in that. There's real gratitude in recollection. There's real gratitude reaching for my mother's voice even when I don't retrieve it. Because I'm reaching for my mother, nonetheless. It reminds me that I am losing a person over, over, and over again, but by losing them, I get to return to the site of their living that I can recall. That is celebratory.

—Hanif Abdurraqib, "When You Lose a Loved One . . ."

Before I really knew it, the searching, sampling, selection, and reselection I was doing through all the gigabytes of mostly pirated music I was downloading on that Dell computer incited me to add a reading practice to my listening practice. Eventually, I discovered a deciphering practice of how they just maybe part and parcel of the same type of revisitation.

The soothing and soothsaying they offered me gave a hint of James Baldwin: "You think your pain and your heartbreak are unprecedented in the history of the world, but then you read." I had come across something more powerful than me, yes, but maybe just powerful enough for, or maybe from, my city.

In the music, found both through the page and through the speaker, sound provided me the will and temporary tools to witness and seize the *moment of truth*, like Guru and Premier said it would. And it became even more real. Through the desperately needed but certainly not always welcome intervention of many friends, I may have also learned, relative to some, how to better understand when those rappers and authors were lying to themselves in those records and between the lines of those pages. Which, more honest to say is, to me-myself learning I held and probably was already practicing the capacity of lying to myself too. I would only be able to tell by being willing to face, revisit, and revise the soundtrack of my city in my own life. I would need to get ready to stay ready.

Seizing the moment of truth had to be more than what was happening out there, but attending to those weighty contradictions, those necessary call-ins for fighting revolutions within yourself too. Toni Cade Bambara reminded me, reminded Us, that the spontaneous simplicity of the first question is really knowing whether we want to be well.

Rock, within that sailing, open boat space that existed from the physical loss of my parents, I was certainly searching, and sampling, and selecting, and reselecting to produce something like a collage that in some ways could be my own healing, because I knew I wanted to be well. I, at least, intended to strive to live as if this was so and to fail up in the good-faith process of doing so.

It was the answer I needed. I know I couldn't have given it to myself. It had to come from my city. It must have. That's how I know we know that we can *soundfeel* it out.

> *Collaging is a historical practice of Black imagination. It has helped us to envision unfathomable futures in the face of violence and uncertainty. It has been a creative way to love each other even though we haven't been shown care, to express the depths of our experiences even when no one ever asked how we felt, to give evidence to all the things unseen.*
>
> —Sasha Bonét, "Reimagining Black Futures"

Rock, collaging became about seizing moments of truth from here and there, reflecting them in my creative expression, constructing a little stairway back to a place, maybe my city, that felt and knew I was still being mothered, just a bit more revolutionary and plural through the hearts and hands of the collective village.

From the music to the books to the everyday, Black village storytelling gathered walking through West Philly and North Philly and Chester too, there remains that dungeon-shaking *quickening capacity for survival* that refuses and refutes the bounds of wretched predicament we may find ourselves presently in.

The underlying truths of our complex personhood teach us that while we may be walled in on all four sides, we can still build up. I challenged myself; I strived and strive to live the lasting conviction of those essential truths I claimed from those songs and those books and those stories, maybe more specifically the true performance of those songs and stories as I *felt* them. Like the *feeling* radically essential for improvisatory invention.

Rock, as my homie Ashon says, wrestling with *conviction* offers Us that through repeated practice, we may allow essential truths to inform and revise our postures, and just maybe become our default. These essential truths of lived experience are not just to be called on in the difficult moments, but in the beauty of the everyday.

Rock, Ali Siddiq says a genius ain't nothing but being able to recall who you need in the moment you require.

In that way, I think about the presence of what such a method of intentional living amounts to for me, a platform to start and explore, to strive and revisit my ever-evolving yet always already present city of Us. The village of my city raised me, and I discovered my generation's obligation may just lay within ensuring that this village survived for someone else to trace its footsteps.

Rock, I'm saying if we know that the city need something—even if we don't know what the *different* is—it's that we need Us to realize we are indeed all entangled in this messy, improvised, practice-based, pluralizing process that makes my city our city. Our city is a multiverse and marvel of Black aliveness all unto itself and we must learn to walk upright in it.

Better yet, maybe when we realize we are all exploring our insides and searching out there for an authentic note, a redemption song, we'd be able to practice differently. Not perform, but truly practice, until that process of revision and conviction becomes our default. We will always remain not no better than what we practice.

Rock, just maybe it's our duty to revise ourselves into modeling the responsibility that is required to answer my city, our city's call for providing something different. Like I said when we first started, I know our ancestors already sent the information to answer your—and now our—promise, proposition, and prayer.

At some point, Rock, somewhere all up in my Black-ass interior, *they who gave me life* were freed to be now attributed new and old kind of fictions, which is to say truths. Usable truths possibly easier to sustain disbelief about when you do not have to navigate some Black body's real world human presence.

Just maybe, in being a Black boy babychild of my city losing my parents who were both of this city too, their feeling—to me, within me—possibly became slight misduplications of an essential pattern. They became plural, much more expansive than what I had known, maybe a bit more than I'd ever really know.

They who gave me life became a secret composite of stories, a hidden plot in the Wynter of America that I earned through hard-to-earn Black study and struggle for which I could not count on being able to return to an individuated source.

Rock, I don't know how much of my perception now could be attributed to my (re)memory of then—*they* and them? How much should be attributed to my imagination running away with me?

Rock, Toni Morrison says we will always and forever keep mixing them up. Get used to it, like the flow of the Mississippi River.

And let's keep it all the way real—how much of the lost tapes of my imagination could I claim to be original ideas anyway?

These structures of *feeling* we navigate daily on these tidalectic currents will forever produce some slippery slopes. Growing feels like there's always a present inheritance that I can't stop from coming ashore and yet I know won't ever be fully traced. I can't call it. Can't expect resolution, yet I refuse to be squarely satisfied on this tragic triangular road.

What I am attempting to say, I suppose, is that it has in some meaningful ways remained blurry and difficult for me to walk the line between my own lived histories and those otherwise-plots that come to me in trying to really, really be there with my city. With our people. With Us.

And that of this village that I and all my cousins are related to somehow in this city; all who were thrown into this place and this history without a choice, and yet must claim some responsibility for keeping the secrets of survival alive for our lost generation of liberators to come.

Rock, in these stories I been collecting, and these images from my brother karim brown, I too listened throughout this process of preparing to talk with you. I was reminded that I have been, and may always remain, in the process of figuring out who *they who give me life* are through the incessant, imaginative, improvisatory selection and reselection of my ancestors in my city, which is kinda our city.

Learning that they—my ancestors, the residents of my city, and maybe me too—might just be one and the same. The borders might not be natural but forced, colonially so.

I'm forever processing not who and where they were or where we were, though of course, we know them spots too. But challenging myself and others of my city, which is our city, to notice *who they be now and where we presently are*, as we will indeed live a future with them. I don't see a future without them. I don't see a future without "*they who give us life*" tatted on Us.

Rock, I may just have to make peace with collaging together parts of them, endlessly creating myself and my city from all the stories I've been blessed to witness, from all the voices and testimonies of ordinary people that I cherish and archive as having carved a way for Us to once and for all get by, get over, and get out.

The Black Radical Tradition is a constantly evolving accumulation of structures of feeling whose individual and collective narrative arcs persistently tend toward freedom. It is a way of mindful action that is constantly renewed and refreshed over time but maintains strength, speed, stamina, agility, flexibility, balance. The great explosions and distortions of modernity put into motion—and constant interaction—already existing as well as novel understandings of difference, possession, dependence, abundance. As a result, the selection and reselection of ancestors is itself part of the radical process of finding anywhere—if not everywhere—in political practice and analytical habit, lived expressions (including opacities) of unbounded participatory openness.

—Ruth Wilson Gilmore, "Infrastructures of Feeling"

Art ain't nothing but structured feelings.

—Jack Whitten

I ask you because you are an artist, ________, and because sometimes your singing achieves what the best art accomplishes. A song you sing creates a space with different rules, different possibilities. A space opens that doesn't exist until a listener tunes in and hears your voice, a sudden space that may disappear the very next instant but changes that instant, too, no doubt, and it doesn't matter that the previous moment and the ones before remain whatever they were and lock a person down with unforgiving, unalterable rules and possibilities. None of that matters when I experience the undeniable presence, the unique truth a particular song can deliver—your song, '_____,' my best example—because then I know time, my time, my life is always more than it appears to me. Didn't that voice, that snatch of music just remind me that there's more in any moment, more to the life I think I'm caught up in, than I can ever know, ever understand, ever come to terms with, make peace with, survive, so much more and more and different and other than it had seemed an instant before the music. If I listen, if I let it be, let it alone, just listen to the music while it delivers inklings and intimations of things very different than I thought they were, are, and sometimes I do go there, into a different space, thank you, thank you, the music reveals, that other, more than possible place, and I go there, can't help myself, because I need it, need help so much, I do, I do, I yearn, I hear the music and nothing is what it was an instant before or ever after, maybe, if I listen, keep believing, learning my life is less than nothing and also perhaps a tiny, tiny bit more than everything I believed I already knew, every damned body already knows, if I really listen, let myself hear when a song speaks.

—John Edgar Wideman, "Arizona"

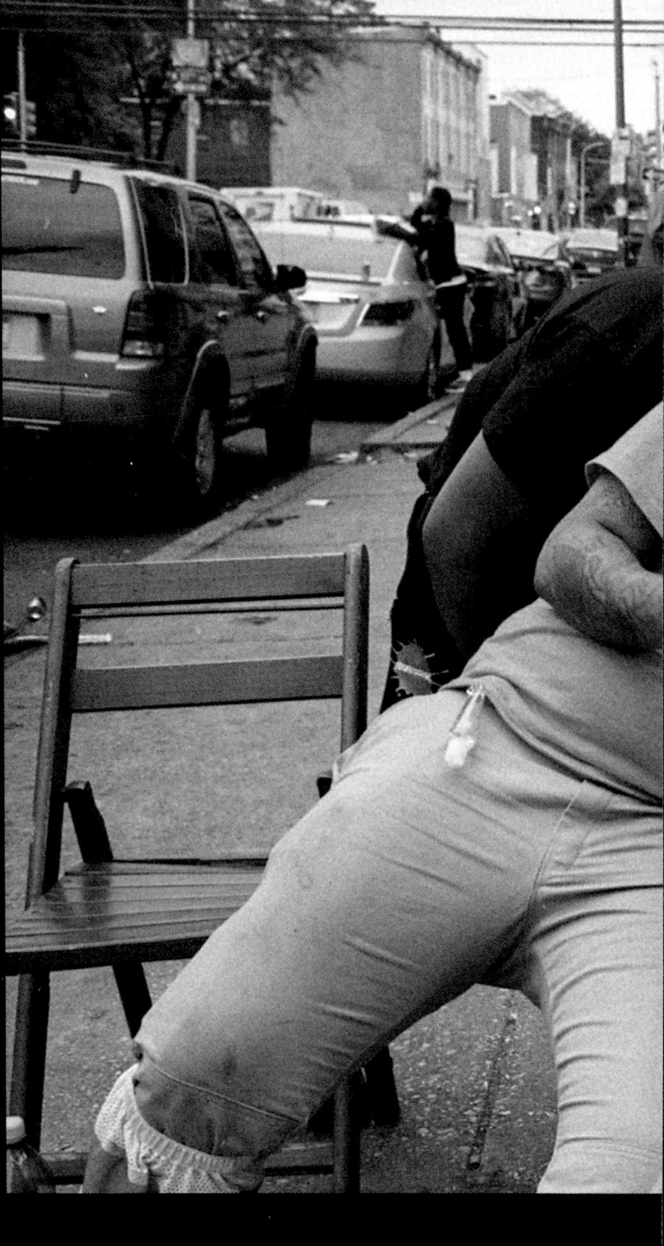

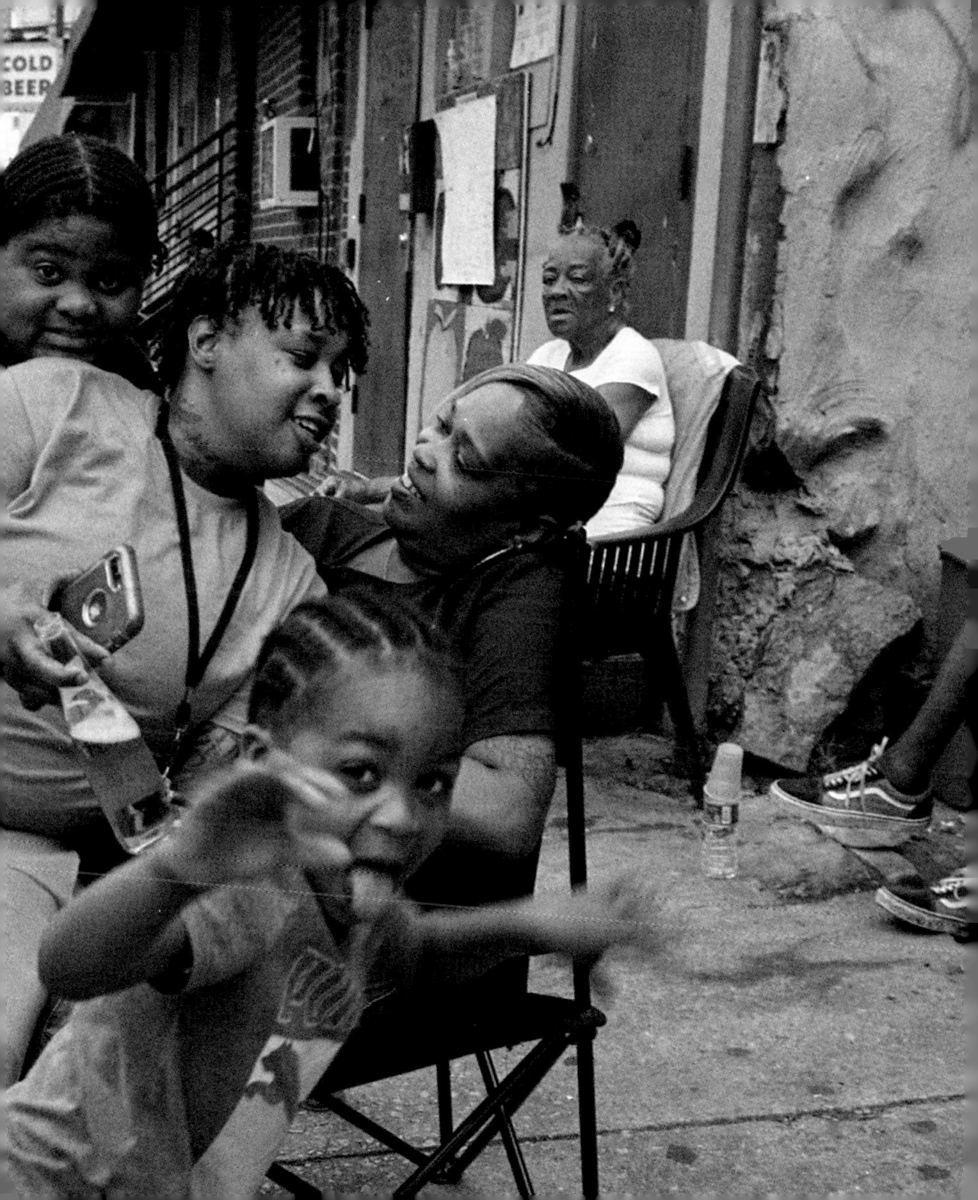
COLD
BEER

every day we lit / free da real

The dream ain't die, only some real niggas.

—Pusha T, "40 Acres"

Rock, thank you. Seriously. This has meant everything to me. I had been meaning to reach out to you for a minute; I mean, since 2022 honestly, after learning of your untimely transition.

That was a wild week in Philadelphia. You know the video was all up and down the timeline. I couldn't watch it. I still don't wanna see it. I don't think it should be in circulation. But you know how we be on the post-Worldstar internet.

That week, I was holding down my volunteer responsibilities at the Robeson House, and my homie Tafari was hosting these Thursday evening porch sessions. Yeah, man, we was on Paul Robeson's porch listening to you. If Uncle Paul only knew the type of music I be playing at high volume in his sister's living room.

Something miraculous occurred that night man, and it never left me. See, I was supposed to be beginning to write up my dissertation that weekend, focused on the story circles I had previously hosted with mostly neighborhood elders in West Philly. But as I checked in at this hotel off South Street, locking in for a productive weekend away from the daily demands, all I could think about was you. Or not just you, but you and your question for Us.

I stay with my Bluetooth speaker on me for these synesthetic staycations, as I believe every piece of writing deserves a proper soundtrack. And I insisted on sitting with the song where I first met you, back when I still lived on Diamond Street in that first-floor apartment. This was my offering to myself that evening, somehow believing that these words spilling out of me would be useful to that dissertation project.

If you've never heard PnB Rock's *My City Need Something*, stop reading this now and do the knowledge. Content warning: loss, grief, police violence.

> *I swear my city need a better way / And I don't think there's nothing left to say / I wrote this song cuz I know just how it feels / To lose somebody you love and that's real . . . I swear we need something different but I don't know what it is.*

These are the timeless lyrics of Rakim Hasheem "PnB Rock" Allen, whose rap moniker honors the Germantown neighborhood intersection of East Pastorius and Baynton Streets upon which he established his reputation as hustler, playboy, and Uptown's native son. After a half-decade of achieving multiplatinum success on the national urban music scene, he was tragically murdered in Los Angeles, California on Monday, September 12, 2022, while out with his girlfriend at the legendary Roscoe's House of Chicken 'N Waffles.

I was rocked. This was a younger man than me that I recognized evolving in real time. The restaurant he helped open, North Philly's Burger Lane, was a delivery lifeline for me and my then-girlfriend, now wife. The music itself echoed the innovations of street language, like Philly's *nation language*. The euphemism "no cap" became "no kizzy" with PnB. He had a certain familiar, yet unique, charismatic bounce to him. An old friend of mine from high school was able to produce a record for him, leading him to achieve his first major label placement and realizing a dream we thought impossible from where we were from. PnB's death occurred the same week I was slated to begin writing, moving forward from the outlined chapter on the role(s) of Black music in Philadelphia as an expressive fugitive archive of Black social life in Philadelphia. If there was anything I could do, I could make a commitment, a promise echoing Kendrick Lamar (2013), that enlivens the praxis of what a Black fugitive archive must do. *The hope that at least one of you will sing about me when I'm gone*. This is the orientation of Christina Sharpe's (2016) "wake work," the call we must answer to defend our dead so that death may never have the final word on Black existence: "The power of the wake . . . is the important work of sitting [together] in the pain and sorrow of death as a way of marking, remembering, and celebrating a life." It is where we insist on Black being.

I first learned about PnB Rock after moving into an apartment in North Philadelphia in 2013, and not shortly after, feeling the echoes of his debut *Real Nigga Bangaz* mixtape blasts its way from the streets through my front window. This was the beginning of his rise to becoming one of the most successful Philadelphia hip-hop artists of his generation. Before he owned the summer of 2017 alongside YFN Lucci with "Everyday We Lit." At that time, PnB was self-admittedly troubled, *fucked up*, on the verge of homelessness, and embracing a fever dream to utilize music as a means of hustling his way into self-sufficiency, growing tired of the promised pitfalls of the illicit economies of Uptown.

Right as he was putting his finishing touches on the highly awaited follow-up *RNB2*, he found himself in prison again, thrown back behind bars for violating probation by leaving his halfway house without permission. Yet, as he discussed in subsequent interviews, he made a promise to himself that this time would be his last. As his songs blew up on local radio to ever greater fanfare, he utilized his commissary funds into renting an exploitatively overpriced Casio keyboard from the prison. He got himself a notebook and pen, spending time writing and practicing some of the hooks and verses that, once he returned home, provided the skeleton foundation of his major record label debut. The prophecy he set over his life would come to be true. Not only did he stay home, he also leveraged his stardom to join in with local organizing efforts to bring others unjustly sentenced home too. "Free da Real," as he said.

RNB2 was released to the world in 2014 while he was still doing a four-month sentence for violating his probation, and the record took off in Philadelphia and beyond. One of the immediate standouts was the mournful "My City Need Something," which is driven by PnB's melodic blues shoutout of a city besieged by persistent gun violence over a somber mid-tempo Superstar Beats production. Interspersed within the record, audio sampled from various local news reports details the fatal inventory of mass shootings that occur at many intersections of Black leisure across North Philadelphia. The lyrics, richly delivered in everyday Philly speak, encapsulate the tantamount grief and unresolved trauma of generation(s) of Black Philadelphia youth besieged by intra-communal violence, the pervasive effects of organized abandonment, and the overall climate of anti-Black racism. Trapped by "trap economics," as Clyde Woods might say. And, just as PnB notes in the record, the police are there to oversee the genocide on layaway plan.

Years later, PnB would tell an interviewer from *The Fader*: "If I listen to that song, I'll cry." I, too, admittedly cried to that record before, on nights driving through the city after being availed of news of another Black life being lost. The tragic news of PnB's murder returned the tears and the grief.

> *And I don't know what it is but my city need something / People killing people over nothing / I swear it's like every day I wake up / Man I hear something like / Man I miss my brother / Rest in peace my hitter / Man they took my sister / I swear we need something different but I don't know what it is . . .*

—

The third edition of "Third Thursdays" at the Paul Robeson House & Museum took place on September 15, 2022. Third Thursdays, conceptualized by Events Coordinator Tafari Robertson, is a simple event in structure. We bring out the PA system on the porch at the corner of 50th and Walnut Streets, and additionally, a table of refreshments and (cheap) wine for the adults. The gathering is meant to be an opportunity for informal relationship-building amongst our neighbors, friends, and those wanting to learn more about our ongoing programming.

You see, the month before, Tafari realized that the PA system could also double as a karaoke system, if you simply cut on the attached wireless mics and used the aux cord connected to somebody's YouTube. Travis Scott, Beyonce, Drake, and others made appearances through the multigenerational voices of our ragtag crew for the night. A month later, as we were finishing up a book discussion on Roxanne Dunbar-Ortiz's *Settler Colonialism* for what it meant to be in solidarity with local Indigenous sovereignty struggles, we planned to run Third Thursdays back with the neighborhood.

Around 9:00 p.m., a foursome of high school-age Black boys who got the last one poppin' just so happened to be circling the block. "Yo, we performing again?" they shouted from the street corner.

"We got y'all," we responded, waving our hand for them to join us on the porch. There was a moment of shared recognition as they entered to where we stood, accepting the mics in hand. "Give us some PnB! *Selfish*?! *Feelings*?! Nah, give us *My City Need Something*!!"

We searched up the record on YouTube (as it still remains unavailable on music streaming platforms, which is to say, it primarily lives on by those who must search for it beyond PnB's most accessible catalog) and turned the mics on for the youngbouls. We held a mournful smile, recognizing the heaviness of what was about to happen, yet remaining anchored within a celebratory mode of just how incredible it would be for all of Us to perform this record, in unison, honoring the beloved local rapper who we at our various ages watched, clamored for, and championed to national stardom. We only had two mics that night, but it didn't matter. We were gonna perform it collectively. We was gonna sing.

> *The chorus bears it all for Us. The chorus is the vehicle for another kind of story. The chorus propels transformation.*
>
> —Saidiya Hartman, *Wayward Lives, Beautiful Experiments*

Many of us were still reeling from the tragic news which virally spread across the internet on Monday night, even quite gruesomely for some, as cell phone footage autoplayed across timelines showing PnB laying on the ground awaiting the arrival of medical attention. I haven't seen the footage and I don't intend to ever visualize such horror. It don't do nothing for me.

Yet, that night on Third Thursday, as a small but mighty cypher of hoodied-up Black boys and men between ninth grade and thirty something circled up on a West Philly porch over a powered speaker, we found ourselves singing the song he sang for Us (and our brothers, sisters, cousins, friends, etc.) less than a decade ago.

> *We just know how it feels . . . We don't think there's anything left to say . . . We swear we need something different but we don't know what it is.*

This final chapter is dedicated to PnB, written in his honor, a means of highlighting what I term "Philly soul musicking" through the back blocks of Philadelphia. Soul musicking, as a transgenerational Black performance practice, has served as a means to archive the complexity of Black lived experiences and articulate collective visions of *something different*, to reach beyond the terror many Black Philadelphians experience, existing within an anti-Black social order, to pursue what must be collectively *felt* to realize liberated futures beyond where individual words, acts, and individuation itself can take us. We are one. We be Us.

(YOU SAID DON'T FORGET ABOUT U) [x2]
(But how we gone forget about you)
(When you was one of the realest niggas)
(All the time we miss you nigga)
(It's fucked up the life they gave you)

Free my niggas.
Free the whole upstate.

Rakim "PnB Rock" Allen (1991–2022)

Well, I wish I could be like a bird in the sky
How sweet it would be if I found I could fly
Oh, I'd soar to the sun and look down at the sea
And then I'd sing 'cause I'd know, yeah
Then I'd sing 'cause I'd know, yeah
Then I'd sing 'cause I'd know
I'd know how it feels
I'd know how it feels to be free, yeah, yeah
Oh, I'd know how it feels
Yes, I'd know, I'd know how it feels
How it feels to be free, Lord, Lord, Lord, yeah

[fade out]

—Nina Simone

free da real.

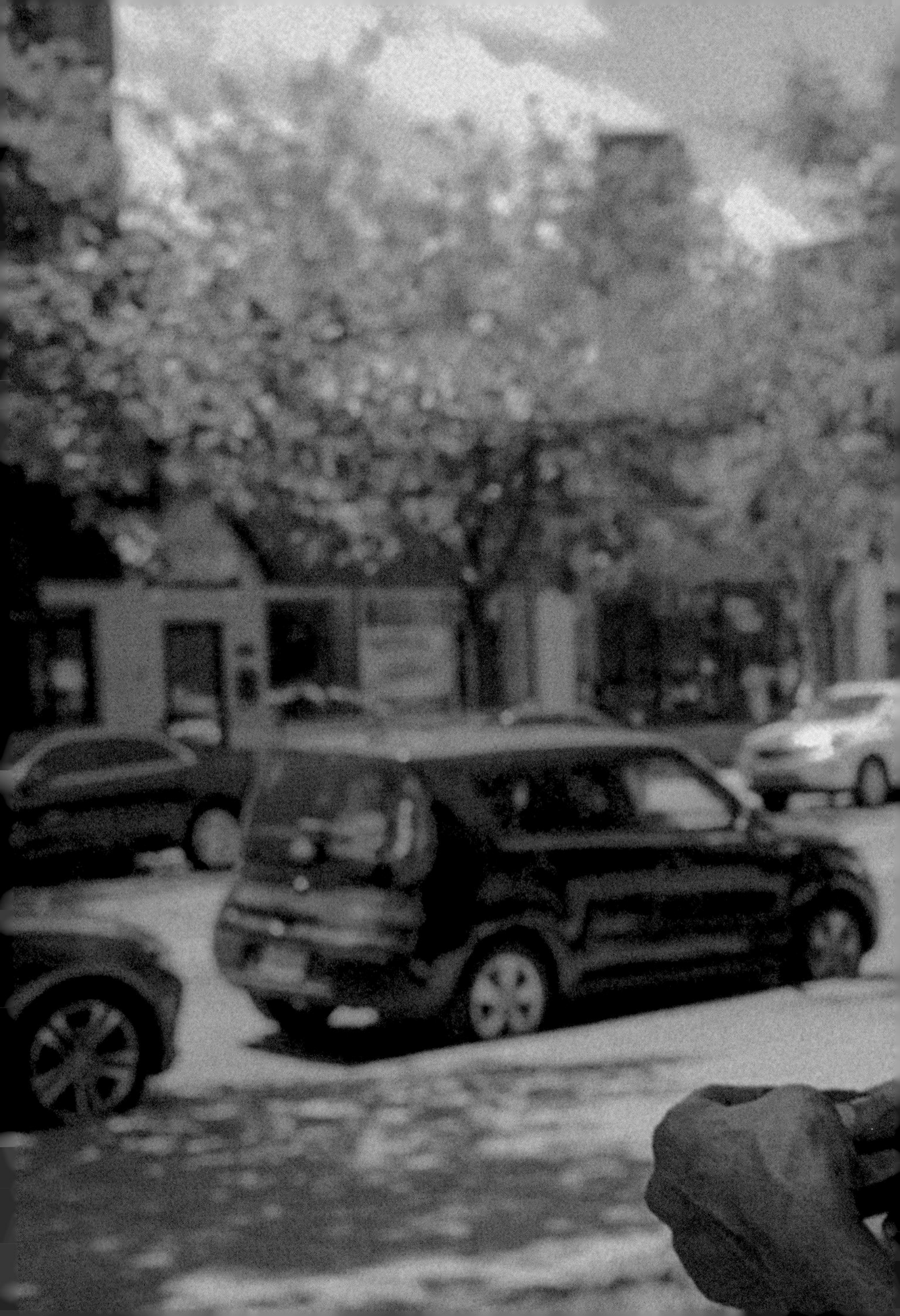

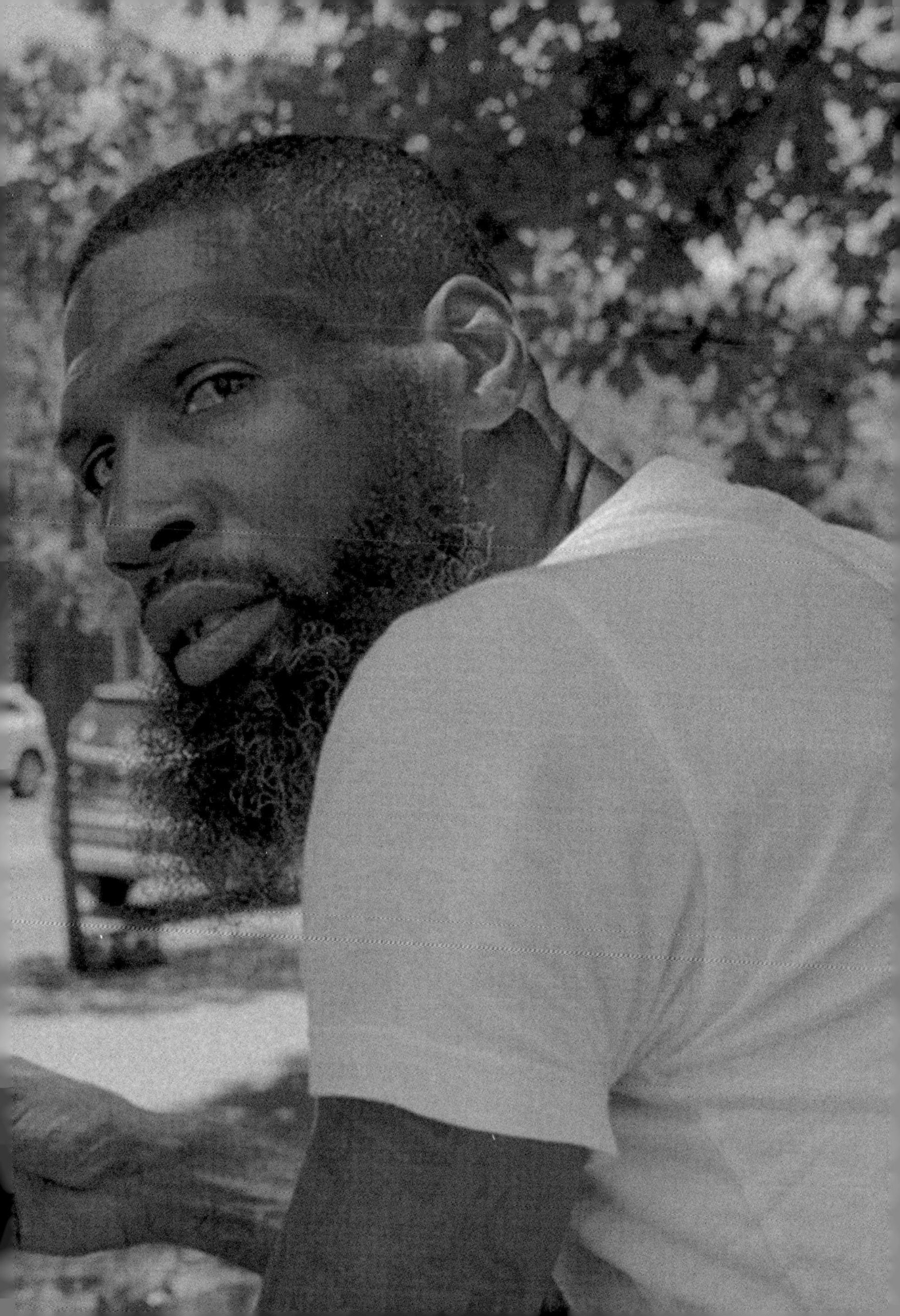

to whom it may concern

To whom it may concern. This goes out, to anybody, who's doing the bullshit—straight up. Yo . . . everybody's calling me, my lawyer, everybody on this "Yo, did you scratch 'such-and-such name,' or 'this, that, and the third,' on the record for a hook?" Y'all keep calling me on that shit—and y'all supposed to be Hip-Hoppers and all that? And letting the industry control the rules of the Hip-Hop world that we made? Y'all need to knock that shit off! That's some greedy-ass, fake bullshit! Knock that shit off, for real! And when that shit come and slap you in the face? That greed? I'ma be right there, laughing at y'all . . . .

And one other thing—What's the deal with you break-record cats, putting out all the original records that we sample from, and snitching by putting us on the back of it, saying we used stuff? You know how that go! Stop doing that, y'all are violatin'—straight up and down! Word up, man, I'm sick of this shit. Y'all muthafuckas really don't know what this Hip-Hop is all about. So, while you keep on faking the funk—we gonna keep on walkin' through the darkness, carryin' our torches. Underground will live forever, baby. We just like roaches—never dying, always living. And on that note, let's get back to the program . . . .

—A PSA from DJ Premier

Bailey, Constance, ed. 2025. *Conversations with Kiese Laymon*. University Press of Mississippi.

Baldwin, James. 2011. *The Cross of Redemption: Uncollected Writings*. Vintage.

Bambara, Toni Cade, and Toni Morrison. 1996. *Deep Sightings and Rescue Missions: Fiction, Essays, and Conversations*. Pantheon Books.

Bambara, Toni Cade, ed. 1970. *The Black Woman: An Anthology*. New American Library, Inc.

Bey, Dawoud, and Brian Ulrich. 2019. *Dawoud Bey on Photographing People and Communities*. Aperture Foundation.

Bracey, John H., Sonia Sanchez, and James Edward Smethurst, eds. 2014. *SOS/Calling All Black People: A Black Arts Movement Reader*. University of Massachusetts Press.

Brooks, Gwendolyn. 2003. *Conversations with Gwendolyn Brooks*. University Press of Mississippi.

Bryer, Jackson R., and Mary C. Hartig, eds. 2006. *Conversations with August Wilson*. University Press of Mississippi.

Campt, Tina M. 2017. *Listening to Images*. Duke University Press.

Césaire, Aimé, and Robin D. G. Kelley. 2000. *Discourse on Colonialism*. Translated by Joan Pinkham. Monthly Review Press.

Césaire, Suzanne. 2012. *The Great Camouflage: Writings of Dissent (1941–1945)*. Edited by Daniel Maximin. Wesleyan University Press.

Chamoiseau, Patrick. 2018. *Slave Old Man: A Novel*. The New Press.

Chamoiseau, Patrick. 1997. *School Days*. Translated by Linda Coverdale. University of Nebraska Press.

Crawley, Ashon T. 2020. *The Lonely Letters*. Duke University Press.

Dumas, Henry. 2021. *Echo Tree: The Collected Short Fiction of Henry Dumas*. Coffee House Press.

Ellison, Ralph. 2002. *Living with Music: Ralph Ellison's Jazz Writings*. Modern Library.

Gilmore, Ruth Wilson. 2022. *Abolition Geography: Essays Towards Liberation*. Edited by Brenna Bhandar and Alberto Toscano. Verso.

Hansberry, Lorraine. "The Negro Writer and His Roots: Toward a New Romanticism." *The Black Scholar* 12, no. 2 (1981): 2–12.

Harney, Stefano, Fred Moten, Denise Ferreira da Silva, and Zun Lee. 2021. *All Incomplete*. Minor Compositions.

Hartman, Saidiya. 2020. *Wayward Lives, Beautiful Experiments*. W.W. Norton & Company.

Henderson, Stephen. 2025. *Black Saturation: Selected Works of Stephen E. Henderson*. Edited by Hazel Arnett Ervin, E. Ethelbert Miller, Phillip M. Richards, and Emily Ruth Rutter. University Press of Mississippi.

hooks, bell. 2025. *All About Love: New Visions*. William Morrow & Company.

Jones, Gayl, and Michael S. Harper. "Gayl Jones: An Interview." *The Massachusetts Review* 18, no. 4 (1977): 692–715.

Jordan, June, and Rachel Eliza Griffiths. 2017. *We're on: A June Jordan Reader*. Edited by Christoph Keller and Jan Heller Levi. Alice James Books.

Lamming, George. 2011. *The George Lamming Reader: The Aesthetics of Decolonisation*. Edited by Anthony Bogues. Ian Randle Publishers.

Laymon, Kiese. 2018. *Heavy: An American Memoir*. Scribner.

Lewis, Thabiti. 2020. *"Black People Are My Business": Toni Cade Bambara's Practices of Liberation*. Wayne State University Press.

Lovelace, Earl. 2004. *Salt: A Novel*. Persea Books.

Lovelace, Earl. 2003. *Growing in the Dark: Selected Essays*. Edited by Funso Aiyejina. Lexicon.

Marshall, Paule. "From the Poets in the Kitchen." *Callaloo* 18, no. 18 (1983): 22.

McKittrick, Katherine. 2021. *Dear Science and Other Stories*. Duke University Press.

Morrison, Toni. 1994. *Conversations with Toni Morrison*. University Press of Mississippi.

Morrison, Toni. 2019. *The Source of Self-Regard: Selected Essays, Speeches, and Meditations*. Alfred A. Knopf.

Moya, Paula ML. "The Search for Decolonial Love: An Interview with Junot Díaz." *Boston Review* 26 (2012).

Myers, Joshua. 2023. *Of Black Study*. Pluto Books.

Neal, Larry, and Allie Biswas. 2024. *Any Day Now: Toward a Black Aesthetic*. David Zwirner Books.

Perry, Imani. 2004. *Prophets of the Hood: Politics and Poetics in Hip Hop*. Duke University Press.

Perry, Imani. 2018. *Looking for Lorraine: The Radiant and Radical Life of Lorraine Hansberry*. Beacon Press.

Reagon, Bernice Johnson. 2001. *If You Don't Go, Don't Hinder Me: The African American Sacred Song Tradition*. University of Nebraska Press.

Richardson, Michael, and Krzysztof Fijalkowski, eds. 1996. *Refusal of the Shadow: Surrealism and the Caribbean*. Verso.

Robeson, Paul. 1978. *Paul Robeson Speaks: Writings, Speeches, Interviews, 1918–1974*. Edited by Philip Sheldon Foner. Brunner/Mazel.

Rowell, Charles H., and Fred Moten. "'Words Don't Go There': An Interview with Fred Moten." *Callaloo* 27, no. 4 (2004): 954–966.

Scott, Julius S. 2018. *The Common Wind: Afro-American Currents in the Age of the Haitian Revolution*. Verso Books.

Spady, James G. "Mapping and Re-Membering Hip Hop History, Hiphopography and African Diasporic History." *Western Journal of Black Studies* 37, no. 2 (2013): 126.

Threadgill, Henry, and Brent Hayes Edwards. 2023. *Easily Slip into Another World: A Life in Music*. Alfred A. Knopf.

Tracy, Steven C., and Etheridge Knight. "A MELUS Interview: Etheridge Knight." *MELUS* 12, no. 2 (1985): 7–23.

Whitten, Jack. 2020. *Notes from the Woodshed*. Edited by Katy Siegel. Hauser & Wirth Publishers.

Wideman, John Edgar. 2021. *You Made Me Love You : Selected Stories, 1981–2018*. Scribner.

Wideman, John Edgar. 1984. *Brothers and Keepers*. Holt, Rinehart and Winston.

West, Cornel, and David Ritz. 2009. *Brother West: Living and Loving out Loud: A Memoir*. SmileyBooks.

Woods, Clyde. 2017. *Development Arrested: The Blues and Plantation Power in the Mississippi Delta*. Verso Books.

Wright, Richard. 2021. *The Man Who Lived Underground: A Novel*. Library of America.

Wynter, Sylvia. 2022. *We Must Learn to Sit down Together and Talk About a Little Culture: Decolonizing Essays, 1967–1984*. Edited by Demetrius Lynn Eudell. Peepal Tree Press Ltd.

about the authors

Christopher R. Rogers, Ph.D is a Philadelphia-based cultural organizer and educator hailing from Chester, PA with more than a decade of experience in supporting radical arts, culture, and community-building. He's a facilitator with the W.E.B. Du Bois Movement School for Abolition & Reconstruction, where he additionally serves as project manager of the renewed *Abolition Journal.* He's also a co-coordinator at the Friends of The Tanner House, incubating a revitalized National Historic Landmark rowhome that Dr. Carter G. Woodson once dubbed the "center of Black intellectual life in Philadelphia." Rogers has also previously published with Common Notions as lead editor for *How We Stay Free: Notes on a Black Uprising* (2022) alongside novelist Fajr Muhammad.

karim brown is a documentary photographer and teacher with roots in North and West Philadelphia. With Black Philadelphia and its people at the forefront of his mind, karim has always been committed to documenting Black folks' ways of knowing and doing. Photography is one way he connects with folks in the community.

about common notions

Common Notions is a publishing house and programming platform that fosters new formulations of living autonomy. We aim to circulate timely reflections, clear critiques, and inspiring strategies that amplify movements for social justice.

Our publications trace a constellation of critical and visionary meditations on the organization of freedom. By any media necessary, we seek to nourish the imagination and generalize common notions about the creation of other worlds beyond state and capital. Inspired by various traditions of autonomism and liberation—in the US and internationally, historical and emerging from contemporary movements—our publications provide resources for a collective reading of struggles past, present, and to come.

Common Notions regularly collaborates with political collectives, militant authors, radical presses, and maverick designers around the world. Our political and aesthetic pursuits are dreamed and realized with Antumbra Designs.

www.commonnotions.org
info@commonnotions.org

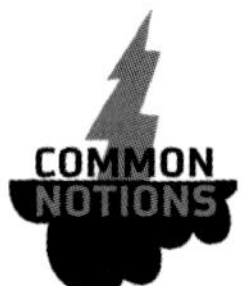